THE PATRIOT
THE OFFICIAL COMPANION

SUZANNE FRITZ & RACHEL ABERLY

CONTENTS

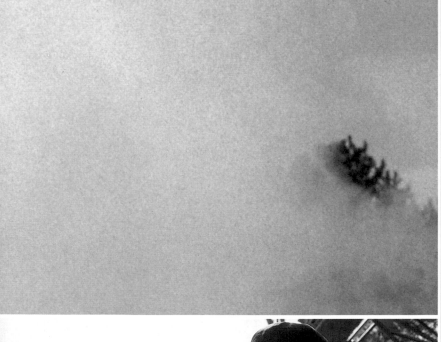

ACKNOWLEDGEMENTS

The authors would like to thank the following people whose help, advice and humor made this book possible: Roland Emmerich, Dean Devlin, Ute Emmerich, Bill Fay, Peter Winther, Dionne McNeff, Maura Wall, Lisa Di Santo, Marc Roskin, Vanessa Jordan, Mel Gibson, Heath Ledger, Jason Isaacs, Mark Gordon, Robert Rodat, Grace Ressler, Cindy Irwin, Ed Russell, Dennis Higgins, Andre Caraco, Jenny Fritz, John Sacchi, Rachel Seltzer, Kristen March, Ken & Brenda Fritz

CREDITS

Director – Roland Emmerich
Executive Producers – William Fay, Ute Emmerich, Roland Emmerich
Producers – Dean Devlin, Mark Gordon and Gary Levinsohn
Written by Robert Rodat
Director of Photography – Caleb Deschanel
Production Designer – Kirk M. Petruccelli
Editor – David Brenner
Music by John Williams
Visual Effects – Stuart Robertson
Costume Designer – Deborah L. Scott
Mel Gibson as Benjamin Martin
Heath Ledger as Gabriel Martin
Joely Richardson as Charlotte Selton
Jason Isaacs as Colonel William Tavington
Chris Cooper as Colonel Harry Burwell
Tcheky Karyo as Major Jean Villeneuve
Rene Auberjonois as Reverend Oliver
Tom Wilkinson as Lord General Charles Cornwallis

Dialogue excerpts from the screenplay written by Robert Rodat

PICTURE CREDITS

Unit Photography – Andrew Cooper
Set/Location Photography – Barry Chusid
Make-Up Effects Photography – Bill Johnson
Smithsonian Institution Photography – Hugh Talman
Digital Effects Imagery – Centropolis Effects
Page 91, bottom – Courtesy of House of Moves

SOURCES

Alden, John R. *A History of the American Revolution.* DaCapo Press, New York, 1969
Bobrick, Benson. *Angel in the Whirlwind.* Penguin Books, New York, 1997
Roberts, Kenneth. *The Battle of Cowpens.* East Acorn Press, New York, 1989
Brittanica.com
Historychannel.com

BURWELL:
This is not a war for the independence of one or two colonies, but for the independence of one nation.

WILKINS: (rising from his seat)
And what nation is that?

Peter Howard, Anne's father, stands up.

HOWARD:
An American nation.

FOREWORD

When I read *The Patriot*, there was no question in my mind that I wanted to direct the film. The story, set during the American Revolution, of an ordinary man torn between protecting his family and his patriotic obligations was a story I wanted to tell. Deciding to direct the film turned out to be the easiest part. With a film of this scope, including themes of such historical importance, special care had to be taken in all areas of production. This proved a challenge on so many levels for every member of the cast and crew. In addition to the inherent difficulties we faced, we had chosen to shoot where these events actually occurred, the Carolinas, so we had to act fast when four hurricanes came barreling down. Despite the

weather, everyone rose to the occasion, motivated in part by a script so good that we knew the potential was there to make a special movie.

Much like the script itself, the production of the movie was multi-layered, requiring each department to pay uncharacteristic attention to detail. In many cases, these details weren't created to stand out but rather the opposite, to create a seamless canvas on which the story could unfold. In creating a book about *The Patriot* we want to give readers some idea of what went into our sets, costumes, props and special effects. It also looks at how some of the most difficult scenes were shot and what it was like to recreate a period in American history that has rarely been seen on celluloid.

Making *The Patriot* was an incredible journey for me in which we took chances, stretching both visually and creatively. In the end, I think we succeeded in creating a special movie. My hope is that *The Patriot* and the hard work of so many has an impact on you.

Roland Emmerich

INTRODUCTION

In 1763, the nine-year French and Indian War ends, leaving Britain in control of Canada and all the territory between the Appalachian Mountains and the Mississippi River. In many ways, the survivors of this long war, the settlers who live on and fought for the land, have stronger ties to it and to each other than to Britain. After years of warfare, these hardy men and women, who collectively make up Great Britain's thirteen colonies in the New World, are ready to return to their ordinary lives in the burgeoning new cities and the countryside.

Benjamin Martin is one of these men. A wily and ferociously effective warrior, he leaves his brutality behind him and goes back to his home in South Carolina. He marries a fine woman who bears him seven children and, under her influence, he trades his violent past for a peaceful future on his sprawling plantation.

But the cost of Pax Britannia is high and the young colonies are increasingly unwilling to pay. A series of taxes are demanded: the Currency, Sugar, Stamp and Quartering Acts come in rapid succession, and the draconian Intolerable Acts follow. The colonists strenuously object to the notion of "taxation without representation" and the concomitant undermining of their

right to self-government. Another conflict, now with Britain, is inevitable.

This time, Benjamin Martin is not so sure. While the British yoke is oppressive, he is not anxious to return to battle for he has different goals now. His wife has died in childbirth, leaving him responsible for his brood of children. Tragedy and the sins of his past have transformed him. A circumspect and taciturn man, his sober façade belies a troubled soul. The horrors of combat haunt him still and the savage acts that won him the admiration of his comrades in the previous war gnaw at his conscience.

His oldest son, Gabriel, has no such doubts. The radical speeches, pamphlets and newsletters coming out of the cities and churches and crossing the colonies make a great impression on the young man. War is coming and the cause, the new and independent country, is just. In defiance of his father, he joins the fight and inadvertently brings conflict right to his family's doorstep.

The emotionally charged adventure *The Patriot* tells the story of how Benjamin Martin, a reluctant hero, is swept into the American Revolution when the war reaches his farm and the British endanger all that he holds most dear. Taking up arms alongside his idealistic patriot son, Gabriel, he leads a rebel American militia into battle against the relentless Redcoat army. In the process, he discovers that the only way to protect his family is to fight for the young nation's freedom.

The film was shot on locations in South Carolina, near the historic Revolutionary War battle sites that would have so affected the lives of Benjamin Martin and his family. Recreating the battles and sweeping landscapes, as well as the bustling city of Charleston, required an active cast and crew, comprised of sixty-three principal actors and ninety-five stunt men, 400 extras and 400 re-enactors. The actors learned the routines of eighteenth-century warfare, as well as the less refined guerrilla combat, and brushed up on their horseback riding in a pre-production boot camp.

Major structures were built to accommodate the drama and the action of the film, including the entire town of Pembroke, the ruins of Cowpens and Benjamin Martin's plantation. For the first time in their history, the Smithsonian Institution served as a liaison to the production to make sure that everything was historically accurate, within the parameters of the movie. The production designer, costume designer, and prop-master agree that this collaboration proved invaluable.

The effects for this film are subtle, unlike the previous films Dean Devlin and Roland Emmerich have done, but posed just as great a challenge, including creating thousands of soldiers, cannonfire and even entire villages.

The movie was an undertaking of great proportion but the team was excited and ready for the challenge. Their travels and travails follow.

PART I
–
THE GENESIS OF *THE PATRIO*

*T*he *Patriot* began in 1996 from an interest in the American Revolution shared by screenwriter Robert Rodat and producer Mark Gordon. The two had previously collaborated in the same capacities on the seminal film *Saving Private Ryan*.

"Bob [Rodat] and I had finished the development of *Saving Private Ryan*. We were trying to decide what we were going to do next. Bob said, 'Why don't we do something set in the American Revolution?'" Gordon remembers. "Growing up in Newport News, Virginia, right outside of Williamsburg and Yorktown, significant historical landmarks of the Revolutionary War were all around – that whole area is filled with them."

Gordon explains that the Revolution itself is not the film's story but rather its backdrop and the catalyst for events that cause the characters, specifically the main protagonist, Benjamin Martin, to examine and, eventually, to completely change his life. "What we ultimately came to thematically is that you can't save your own family unless you are willing to put yourself on the line to save the families of all men. In the story, Benjamin Martin initially believes that the only way to protect his family is to stay out of the war and not become a part of the conflict. What he comes to realize is that the only way he is able to save the smaller part, his family, is to be a part of what is ultimately the larger part, and to fight in the American Revolution on the side of the Patriots. I think these issues are important and I hope they will have resonance for the audience not only in terms of fighting a war but in all aspects of our lives," Gordon says.

Levinsohn agrees, explaining, "What's so great about these types of stories is that they're really everybody's story. It's America's story, the New World story. It's Australia's, it's South Africa's story. It's for anyone who is forced to defend their children and their beliefs."

The shooting script evolved through an osmosis-like process, based on Rodat's fascination with the Revolutionary War. "After *Ryan* I was trying to decide what to write next. One thing I've found in writing is that it is much better to read a lot of books over a long period of time rather than the same number of books over a short period of time. For many years, I had had an interest in World War II and I had also had an interest in the American Revolution. I think that reading books slowly with a lot of space between them and living your life between those books allows the themes and stories to gestate in a way that wouldn't happen if you said, 'I'm going write a movie about X,' and then started to research and write that. From the time I was a kid, the American Revolution always fascinated me. I've never understood why there wasn't a movie that had captured it."

Rodat adds that it wasn't just the battles that intrigued him but the conflict's underlying issues and the terrible choices it presented ordinary people with. "Unlike *Ryan*, *The Patriot* deals with a war fought on the home front. As I have children of my own, it became natural to deal with the effects and repercussions of a conflict like the Revolution; it seemed natural to deal with someone like Benjamin Martin, who has to grapple with competing responsibilities. Actually, that's like *Ryan* too. But in

this case, it is [about] competing responsibilities to family and to principle. There is a line in one draft of the script in which one of the characters says that 'wars are not only fought by childless men, and a man must balance his personal responsibilities against his principles.' And that's in a war that's fought around your home and in your backyard, so it's particularly telling. *The Patriot* is the story of a man who has conflicting responsibilities to this developing nation and to his family. It's a story about how he tries to deal with obligations that are in direct conflict."

Columbia Pictures agreed with Rodat and purchased the screenplay. Their Chairman, Amy Pascal, explains, "We like the story of a man defending his family because it's powerful and universal." After Rodat, Gordon and Levinsohn had developed and polished the screenplay, they searched with Columbia for a filmmaker to direct the project. Instead, they found a filmmaking team, in the form of director Roland Emmerich and producer Dean Devlin. Known for their science fiction spectaculars *StarGate*, *Independence Day* and *Godzilla*, to some Hollywood "cognoscenti" they might have seemed an unlikely choice for *The Patriot*.

Mark Gordon disagrees. "We were looking for a great storyteller. Roland was a director that I had always been very interested in working with. We had been big fans of Roland's and Dean's from *Independence Day* and thought that all of their pictures were terrific. When you are looking for a director, you have two options. You can turn to someone who has done this kind of genre five times before or you can opt to work with someone who is extraordinarily talented and is a great storyteller but hasn't told this particular kind of story. So that was why we were excited about the possibility of Dean and Roland getting involved in this kind of picture, and it has been an incredibly happy and fulfilling collaboration."

As Levinsohn points out, "On some level it took the courage that Benjamin Martin had to have for Roland to do this film. I think it was worthwhile and brave of him to go after this material."

"I think Roland and Dean are going to surprise people," Rodat adds. "They are very thoughtful, well-read men with high aspirations. I'm really pleased with the pairing."

Emmerich and Devlin returned Rodat's compliment during filming. They referred to the script affectionately as "The Book of Rodat." Contrary to what happens on some movie sets, the writer was a welcome frequent visitor and a continuing contributor, adding scenes or honing dialogue as required.

"It really came down to the script for us," Emmerich notes. "I never thought I would make a movie about the American Revolution, but I was so moved by this story, very taken by it."

"We also discovered a little-known aspect of the American Revolution, that aliens actually helped us win. We thought we could focus in on that and bring our expertise to it," Devlin jokes. "No, actually, the script was so powerful and such a beautiful piece of work, challenging and exciting for us. I remember that I was given the script to read over a weekend and I actually started reading it about fifteen minutes before a party I was throwing at my house. It was so engrossing that I couldn't stop reading it, even though I had a house full of people. I got about seventy

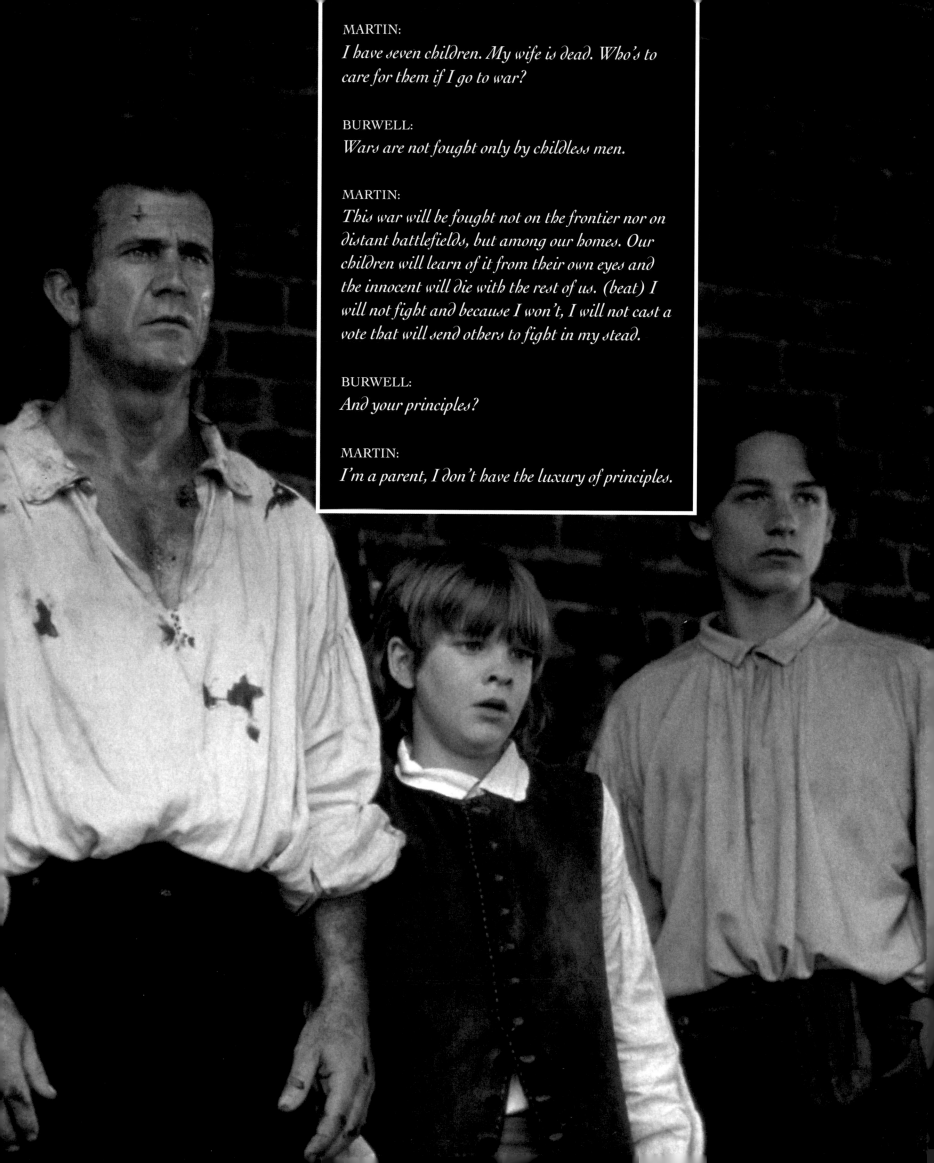

MARTIN:
I have seven children. My wife is dead. Who's to care for them if I go to war?

BURWELL:
Wars are not fought only by childless men.

MARTIN:
This war will be fought not on the frontier nor on distant battlefields, but among our homes. Our children will learn of it from their own eyes and the innocent will die with the rest of us. (beat) I will not fight and because I won't, I will not cast a vote that will send others to fight in my stead.

BURWELL:
And your principles?

MARTIN:
I'm a parent, I don't have the luxury of principles.

pages into the script when I ran to the telephone and called Roland. I said, 'Roland, whatever you're doing, stop. You've got to read this script. It's our next movie.' He promptly said to me, 'I already read it. Finish the script and call me back.' I did and we were both madly in love with it and thought that this was the opportunity of a lifetime."

Gareth Wigan, Co-Vice Chairman of the Columbia TriStar Motion Picture Group recalls that, "What excited *me* was that the filmmaker, who I very much admire, was so excited about it. He wasn't just interested, he immediately seized on it and you could see the light in his eyes. Right away Roland "saw" the film and immediately *The Patriot*, which up to then was simply a very well written script, started to come alive. Roland is a singular director; he's not a director on a list. When there's that sudden meeting of a singular filmmaker with a singular piece of material, there's a passion that I think is like a spark in a tinderbox." Columbia Chairman Amy Pascal agrees and says simply, "Roland was absolutely the perfect director to bring the story to life."

Emmerich, born in Germany ten years after the end of World War II, notes that the screenplay affected him on a visceral and personal level. "There is no escaping something as massive as a war and the story was told in a way that anyone could relate to. I started crying as I read the script, which has happened maybe twice in my life, and that really got me. The American Revolution was a big subject taught in school in Germany because it was one of the only formations of a democratic society since the Ancient Greeks, so I had a real connection to the material," he says.

Devlin adds that the screenplay's humanity, drama and pathos appealed to him, as well as its historical elements. "It's an enormously emotional, compelling story about a father and a son, which I think everyone can relate to, the idea of a father trying to keep his family together. And the idea of setting a film during the American Revolution was fascinating, especially as we moved into the new millennium. It's an interesting time to look back and think about how this country was started. There aren't really a lot of films about that period, about the birth of this

Executive producer Ute Emmerich with Jason Isaacs, who plays Colonel Tavington

country, and we thought it was an amazing chance to show what life was like for a normal person at that time, how ordinary people faced extraordinary circumstances. Beyond its historical elements, though, the story touches you in an incredible way. To have this compelling human drama in an original visual setting, we were compelled to do it."

Once Devlin and Emmerich were on board, there was one significant change: the inspiration for Rodat's lead character. Benjamin Martin had initially mirrored famous American militiaman Francis Marion, but he was subsequently reworked to reflect several men of the war, as well as the fictional moral dilemma. As Devlin explains, "By not tying him down to one person, we were able to make the Benjamin Martin character more of a reflection of the people and events of the period. You walk a very fine line when you adapt something like this. We tried to keep all the events of the movie real to events that happened in the American Revolution. They may not have happened in the same way or in the same place, but the spirit of everything in the film can be drawn from real events all throughout the American Revolution."

While the Revolutionary War was the inspiration for *The Patriot*, and provides its colourful and dramatic backdrop, at the film's center is the story of a man's inner turmoil and a family in crisis, which convinced Mel Gibson to take the role of Benjamin Martin. Gibson explains, "While it is a very big film, at the core of it is a real story with characters that are quite understandable, just ordinary people. I've seen epics and some of them don't touch you because they are these big, sprawling things. They don't reach you on an emotional or human level at all. The more intimate story and just the simple truths of the human experience have to be very clear in order for the epic nature of the film to be worthwhile. That, I think, is what attracted me to this script. The far more important story is the one of the people, the characters – the story of the family, something that everyone can

Filmmaking team Roland Emmerich (left) and Dean Devlin

relate to. And if that works, well, then you can have as many cannon blasts as you like and they mean something."

Roland Emmerich

Roland Emmerich directed and executive-produced *Godzilla*, which he co-wrote with producer Dean Devlin. They worked in the same capacities on the box-office phenomenon *Independence Day*, the fourth highest grossing film of all time. Emmerich helmed 1994's epic science fiction adventure *StarGate*, which he also co-wrote with Devlin. Emmerich's first American film was the 1992 action-adventure hit *Universal Soldier*, starring Jean-Claude Van Damme.

Emmerich began his career in his native Germany. As a youth, he pursued painting and sculpting, studying production design while in the director's program at film school in Munich. His student film, *The Noah's Ark Principle*, went on to open the 1984 Berlin Film Festival. The feature became a huge success and was sold to more than twenty countries.

Subsequently, Emmerich formed his own production company, Centropolis Film Productions, and under its aegis produced *Making Contact* (a.k.a. *Joey*), a film that showcased the young filmmaker's vast knowledge of special effects, and *Ghost Chase*, a comedy he co-wrote with Oliver Eberle. He went on to direct the futuristic action-adventure *Moon 44*, which he co-wrote with Eberle, starring Malcolm McDowell, Michael Pare, Lisa Eichhorn and Dean Devlin. While Devlin was working with Emmerich as an actor in 1989's *Moon 44*, the two found they enjoyed similar movies and Devlin's writing ability impressed the director as much as his acting. Devlin subsequently gave up acting to write and produce movies with Emmerich under his Centropolis Film banner.

Dean Devlin

Before American-born Dean Devlin co-wrote and produced such blockbusters as *Godzilla*, *Independence Day*, and *StarGate*, he was a successful Broadway, television and screen actor.

In addition to his writer/producer duties on *Independence Day*, which has grossed over $800 million worldwide, Devlin also served as second unit director on the film. While working on *StarGate* with Emmerich, he launched the first movie website,

which began a whole new field of motion picture marketing. He executive-produced the science fiction drama series *The Visitor* along with Emmerich, also writing several episodes. He is a partner in Centropolis Entertainment which is a multi-faceted entertainment organization that develops and produces a variety of ventures including film, television, interactive, music and publishing projects.

Mark Gordon

Mark Gordon is a partner with Gary Levinsohn in the Mutual Film Company, which produced the multi-Academy Award®-winning *Saving Private Ryan*. Mutual's recent productions include *Wonder Boys*, Curtis Hanson's follow-up to *L.A. Confidential*, the critically acclaimed Jim Carrey starrer *Man on the Moon*, Mike Nichols' *Primary Colors*, *A Simple Plan*, *Hard Rain* and *The Jackal*. Prior to joining Levinsohn in 1996, he produced *Broken Arrow*, *Speed*, *Pyromaniacs: A Love Story*, *Trial by Jury*, *Swing Kids* and *Fly by Night*, which won the Filmmaker Prize at the 1993 Sundance Film Festival.

Gordon has also produced numerous television projects, including the Emmy Award-winning documentary short *Nothing But the Sun*, a study of the Holocaust as seen through the eyes of children, which he also directed; and *The War Between Classes*, for which he won an Emmy Award for Best Children's Program. He began his producing career with the off-Broadway play *The Buddy System*, which was presented at the acclaimed theater Circle in the Square.

Gary Levinsohn

Before becoming a partner in Mutual Film, Levinsohn executive-produced the international hit *Twelve Monkeys*. He was also responsible for the formation of Bregman/Baer Productions, which produced and co-financed *Carlito's Way* and *The Shadow*. Born and raised in South Africa, Levinsohn served as Vice-President of International Sales at De Laurentiis Entertainment Group before becoming a producer.

Robert Rodat

Screenwriter Robert Rodat received an Academy Award® nomination in 1998 for *Saving Private Ryan*. His previous writing credits convey his unique range. They include co-scripting (with Vince McKewin) Carroll Ballard's family film *Fly Away Home*, starring Jeff Daniels and Anna Paquin in the story of a young girl who raises a flock of geese and helps them migrate home. He had previously co-written (with Steve Bloom) the fantasy adventure *Tall Tale*.

Growing up in New Hampshire, Rodat received a BA in history from Colgate University. He went on to earn an MBA from Harvard and a Master of Fine Arts from the University of Southern California Film School.

Executive producer Bill Fay (center) with Roland Emmerich and Dean Devlin

PART II

–

HEROES AND VILLAINS

Mel Gibson
—
Benjamin Martin

Mel Gibson is not only one of the world's most accomplished actors, but also an Oscar®-winning director and a respected filmmaker. In the course of his career as an actor, he has starred in a wide variety of films, from the extremely successful *Lethal Weapon* series to the spirited Western *Maverick*, from the psychological thriller *Conspiracy Theory* to the historical epic adventure *Braveheart*. Gibson produced, directed and starred in *Braveheart*, which won five Academy Awards® out of ten nominations, including Best Picture and Best Director. His company, Icon Productions, which he created with Bruce Davey, developed and produced *Braveheart*, along with many other movies, including the hit actioner *Payback*, in which he also starred.

Born in upstate New York, Gibson moved with his family to Australia when he was twelve years old. He attended the National Institute of Dramatic Arts at the University of New South Wales in Sydney and began his acting career. Early stage appearances included a part in *Death of a Salesman*.

At the age of twenty-three Gibson was selected by director George Miller for the title role of his movie *Mad Max*. The film became a cult classic, bringing Gibson worldwide recognition. The title role in *Tim* quickly followed. His moving portrayal of a handicapped young man won him critical acclaim and an Australian Film Institute Best Actor Award.

His star continued to rise with the two hit sequels to *Mad Max – The Road Warrior* and *Mad Max Beyond Thunderdome* – along with Peter Weir's *Gallipoli*, which brought Gibson a second Australian Best Actor Award. A few years later, Weir and Gibson again collaborated, this time on *The Year of Living Dangerously*.

The time had come for Gibson to make the move to Hollywood. His first American film was *The River*, but he is best remembered as Danny Glover's infectiously crazy partner Martin Riggs in the *Lethal Weapon* film series. His other films include *The Bounty, Mrs. Soffel, Tequila Sunrise, Bird on a Wire, Air America* and *Hamlet. Hamlet*, directed by Franco Zeffirelli, was the first film to be produced by Gibson's Icon Productions. The role brought him the William Shakespeare Award from the Folger Theater in Washington, D.C. Icon also produced *Forever Young, Immortal Beloved, Airborne* and *Maverick*. In 1993 Gibson made his directorial debut with *The Man Without a Face*, another Icon production in which he also starred. He recently completed Wim Wenders's *The Million Dollar Hotel*. Gibson follows up *The Patriot* with the romantic comedy *What Women Want* for director Nancy Meyers.

The film's lead character, Benjamin Martin, is someone whose life is inexorably altered by the Revolution. A man of contradictions, he is a ruthless guerilla fighter who becomes a pacifist, a responsible provider and a father; now a respected member of his community, his stoicism masks a conscience plagued by remorse and guilt over his violent past. He commits both the sin of commission by his bloody acts in war and the sin of omission when his initial refusal to join in the fight against the British leads his family to tragedy. He is a profoundly troubled person who labors mightily to be a moral man.

Mel Gibson has some experience in playing reluctant heroes, from his roles in the *Mad Max* series to *Braveheart*. He feels that any similarities between *The Patriot* and his previous films, especially *Braveheart*, have much to do with the cyclical nature of history and of human nature in general. "You don't have to go very far to realize that history quickly repeats itself, century by century, decade by decade. Different players but the same story, just playing itself out, all the victories and defeats. Wars are almost always fought for the same reasons. I don't know many people who go to war all that willingly. So that seems to be a natural and truthful reaction.

"I read a book many years ago by Joseph Campbell called *The Hero with a Thousand Faces* in which he identifies archetypal figures such as 'the reluctant hero.' Themes of evil occur in every culture, in every era, so there are some similarities between *The Patriot* and *Braveheart* in terms of truth of themes. These kinds of stories [have been told] since people were dwelling in caves and painting pictures; the ones that hearten us, the ones that make us reach for something divine rather than ordinary. It's that combination of the ordinary and the divine that inspires us and makes something really hit home for us, I think. And those are the kinds of stories that I like."

Screenwriter Robert Rodat concurs and says that his intention was to explore that classic quandary, the ephemeral balance between human frailty and noble aspiration through the Martin character. "I like films that explore both an external conflict, which war clearly gives you, and an intense internal conflict. And I like the idea of writing films in which the clarity of the external conflict is juxtaposed against the murkiness and the difficulty of the internal conflict of the moral questions Benjamin Martin has." The script, I think, has always been held together by this idea of taking a man and putting him on the hot seat. The measure of this man, this character, is the way in which he deals with directly contradictory responsibilities and conflicting moral imperatives. Mel embraced that from the first day."

Producer Mark Gordon adds that Gibson's ability to capture the duality of Martin's nature, coupled with the actor's intrinsic "timelessness," made him the perfect actor for the part.

"There are very few actors who, we believed, the audience would accept in this role. There are a lot of wonderful actors who feel contemporary. It's not that they're not talented, it's just that somehow they don't feel like they belong in 1776. We all had Mel Gibson in mind for the part from the very beginning. We felt that as an actor he was able to play the physicality and the roughness of the character but at the same time give the

character enormous humanity and great heart. One of the things about the Benjamin Martin character is that he has two sides: the side that has been tamed by his dead wife and the side that is very, very brutal and tough, as a fighter and a soldier. It is hard to find an actor who can play both sides of the role convincingly and also credibly be of the time, in this case the American Revolution."

Roland Emmerich says, "It was a joy to work with Mel. He was very committed to concentrating on the acting and he is the most humble person there is. He has no ego, in terms of how he interacts with the actors and the crew. I think he felt comfortable with us and the best thing we could do was give him the room to act, to create and define this character."

The result was that Mel went above and beyond the call of duty, surprising the crew every day. Executive producer Ute Emmerich recalls, "We were going to shoot in forty frames per second, which results in slow motion, so Mel said, 'Let's have the cameras roll at normal speed, because I can do the slow motion.' We did it and it turned out great."

Devlin echoes these sentiments, adding, "The choices Mel makes as an actor in this film are incredibly brave. He's willing to go to very dark places within his own psyche and expose them on screen if they're right for the character. It's both disturbing and compelling, because you feel like you're looking at something incredibly private within his performance."

Despite the South Carolina media's determination to describe Gibson's character as a cinematic incarnation of a local hero, the famed guerrilla fighter Francis Marion, Rodat emphatically says that Benjamin Martin is an amalgam of several such warriors, and not one in particular. "Our Benjamin Martin has liberal amounts of Thomas Sumter, Andrew Pickens, Daniel Morgan, and even Elijah Clark, as well as Francis Marion. We found very early in the process that our aspirations for the movie were different from the story of Francis Marion. Although he is certainly an element of our character, he is one of a number of elements," he explains.

Each man provided pivotal pieces to the character of Benjamin Martin, who is known as "The Ghost" in the script, because of his ability to ferociously strike and disappear.

Martin's slippery elusiveness is reminiscent of Marion, who would attack the British and retreat into the swamps, earning him the sobriquet "The Swamp Fox." However, his independent spirit, his talent for recruiting men to join his militia, and his effective guerrilla campaign reflect Sumter, a cunning fellow called "The Gamecock," whose wily maneuvers drew the King's troops into ambushes and whose overall harassment cut off British supplies. Like Martin, Sumter had to be wooed into war, although for a different reason. Sumter and his forces would be of help to Major-General Nathaniel Green but Sumter was stubborn and preferred to fight on his own without any interference.

Morgan had his own unique strategy which included a 1000-strong force of light infantry, riflemen, regular army and militia, the latter of which led the crucial colonial victory at the Battle of Cowpens under Pickens. After this win at Cowpens, Sumter, Pickens, Marion and the militia became even more important to the overall campaign because there was no organized American army in the Carolinas or Georgia. As a result, they actively fought the Loyalists throughout the region.

Elijah Clark, like Benjamin Martin, headed his own militia, although his troops hailed from Georgia. Along with Pickens and his men, Clarke contributed to one of the few early Patriot victories in the South, at Kettle Creek. Kettle Creek particularly illustrated the familial nature of the conflict, presaging the Civil War in that it compelled brother to take up arms against brother, father against son, as the colonists became Patriots or Loyalists. Pickens and Clarke, along with Colonel John Dooley, set their South Carolina and Georgia militias against a group of North Carolina militia en route to join the British at Augusta.

Gibson describes Benjamin Martin as an erstwhile "hell-raiser" who, despite his apparent "civility," can't quite dodge his brutal past. The character's uneasy balance between the man he was and the one he aspires to be intrigued the actor.

"He was a kind of savage during the French and Indian War and when we meet him, he is trying to maintain a simple lifestyle and stay out of trouble. He's tempered by his past and by having children, and by remorse for the sins he thinks he has committed during the war.

"There's a sense of foreboding through the entire film that has to do with his transgressions and his remorse for them. His conscience bothers him. He's motivated by the fear that he could easily regress into his former brutality and that his sins and transgressions will come back to haunt him, that he will have to pay a moral debt that will mean losing what he has. His family and his farm, the new life he has built, he just wants to hang on to all of it so hard that it starts slipping through his fingers. Eventually, he finds that he has to either get into the conflict or do nothing and watch as his family is torn apart. He says at one point that 'the war will be fought in our backyards' and literally that happens to him," Gibson explains.

He adds that the character's vulnerability interested him, and it is this characteristic that differentiates Benjamin Martin from *Braveheart*'s William Wallace. "The similarity is that they were both fighting for independence in a revolution, but their motives for ultimately joining the war are very different. Both are initially reluctant to fight, but Martin hesitates out of fear. He is terribly afraid because of his own past and the karmic retribution that might result. He has a lot to lose now. He has seven children and that makes him very vulnerable."

Because of Martin's fears and ambivalence, he doesn't initially embrace the coming revolution and, Gibson points out, the true "Patriot" of the movie is not the father but the son. "In fact, his oldest son is the Patriot. After that, Martin's motive for engaging in battle is just about protecting his home and his family."

Emmerich adds, "There's an assumption that everybody's patriotic and not everybody is. This movie is called *The Patriot*, but Benjamin Martin is not a Patriot. He knows what war is and feels that we should avoid it under all circumstances. That's quite different than other men from history. He's reluctant and that gives him a whole other feel. Everyone else around him is more patriotic than he is.

"In the end, he fights not for himself but for his children. That was an aspect of the script that got to me. He fights for more than himself, for more than just revenge. Destiny has another plan for him. In the end, he becomes a kind of Patriot but it's not black and white – there are so many layers. He carries the flag at the end to rally the troops not so much out of patriotism but as the symbol of his personal struggle."

SCREENWRITER ROBERT RODAT DREW EXTENSIVELY FROM HISTORICAL FIGURES, BATTLES AND LAWS FOR MANY ELEMENTS OF THE FILM, CREATING NOT ONLY SIGNIFICANT PARALLELS BUT ALSO DIVERSIONS BY LOOKING AT SOME OF THESE PEOPLE AND EVENTS.

BENJAMIN MARTIN WAS A COMPOSITE OF SEVERAL HEROES OF THE AMERICAN REVOLUTION, INCLUDING FRANCIS MARION, DANIEL MORGAN AND THOMAS SUMTER.

ALL WERE MILITIA FIGHTERS WHO USED GUERRILLA TACTICS AND THEIR EXPERTISE IN THE SWAMPLANDS TO HELP SECURE AMERICA'S VICTORY OVER THE BRITISH.

—

FRANCIS MARION

Francis Marion was born 1732 in Winyah, South Carolina. He gained his first military experience fighting against the Cherokee Indians in 1759 and went through the ranks until he was commissioned a captain in 1775 during the South Carolina Provincial Congress.

He was nicknamed "The Swamp Fox" by the British for his elusive strategies during the American Revolution. He would slip away to the swamps which he knew well, gather his ragtag team of men, and lead violent raids on the British. With their surprise tactics and rapid movements through the marshy terrain, Marion and his militia, known as Irregulars, often defeated larger numbers of British troops. Toward the end of the Revolution, Marion's team relied heavily on these guerrilla tactics and were successful in driving the British General Charles Cornwallis from the Carolinas and to defeat at Yorktown, Virginia. For his efforts, Marion received the thanks of Congress and was appointed brigadier-general. After the war, he served in the Senate of South Carolina from 1782 to 1790. He died at the age of sixty-three in 1795 in Berkeley County, South Carolina.

Today a National Forest and a university, both in South Carolina, carry Marion's name.

—

DANIEL MORGAN

Daniel Morgan was born in Hunterdon County, New Jersey, in 1736. He became well known as a master of raids, an excellent rifleman and a symbol of someone who would risk anything for the American cause.

Morgan moved to Virginia in 1753 and was commissioned a captain of Virginia riflemen at the outbreak of the Revolution. He accompanied General Benedict Arnold to Canada and in the assault on Quebec he and his riflemen stormed deep into the city, where they were locked in and forced to surrender. On his release, he joined General Horatio Gates and took part in both Battles of Saratoga, New York, in 1777.

Morgan resigned from the army in 1779, partly because of ill-health, but after the monstrous American defeat at the Battle of Camden, South Carolina, in 1780 he agreed to rejoin Gates at Hillsborough, North Carolina. He was made a brigadier-general and took command of a corps, setting his sights on slowing down the advance of General Cornwallis in the south. To do so, he progressively retired northward and then turned suddenly to confront the British troops at Cowpens on January 17, 1781. The tactic was a great success, with Morgan winning a brilliant and unexpected victory over a larger force led by Colonel Banastre Tarleton.

Morgan was a Federalist representative in Congress from 1797 to 1799. He died in 1802 in Winchester, Virginia, at the age of sixty-six.

—

THOMAS SUMTER

Thomas Sumter was born in Hanover County, Virginia, in 1734. A legislator and officer in the American Revolution, he was known as the "Carolina Gamecock" for his leadership of troops against British forces in North and South Carolina.

He served in the French and Indian War before moving to South Carolina. He became a brigadier-general of state troops in North Carolina after he escaped the fall of Charleston in 1780. He had successes over the British at Catawba and Hanging Rock, but was beaten at Fishing Creek. He defeated Mayor Wemyss at Fishdam Ford and repulsed Colonel Tarleton at Blackstock in November 1780.

Following the war, Sumter served in the U.S. House of Representatives from 1789 to 1793 and 1797 to 1801, and in the U.S. Senate from 1801 to 1810. He was the last surviving general officer of the Revolution. He died at age ninety-eight in 1832 in South Mount, South Carolina.

Fort Sumter in Charleston Harbor was named after him.

HEATH LEDGER
—
GABRIEL MARTIN

Heath Ledger recently starred in *10 Things I Hate About You*, the update of Shakespeare's *The Taming of the Shrew* set in the vicious world of high school. American audiences first saw the Australian-born actor on the Fox adventure series *Roar*, which, ironically, was shot in Queensland, Australia, near his home in Perth. He began his acting career there, enrolling in a local theater company at the age of ten. He soon began to get roles on several Australian television series, while continuing his stage work as a member of the Globe Shakespeare Company and the Midnight Youth Acting Company. He subsequently completed co-starring roles in several Australian independent films, including *Black Rock*, *Paws* and *Two Hands*, which screened at the Sundance Film Festival. Ledger stars in the fantasy feature *A Knight's Tale* for Columbia Pictures and director Brian Helgeland.

Heath Ledger plays Benjamin Martin's oldest son, Gabriel, the youth who in many ways becomes his father's teacher. "I thought it would be interesting to have the teacher in this case be the son," Rodat says. "Gabriel is a decent, moral guy, and he wears that mantle of principle and responsibility more easily than his father does. Gabriel has the moral certitude that is afforded him by having been raised by a more civilized mother, but his father is a man of the frontier. Benjamin Martin grew up in a rougher time than his son did, when violence and occasional brutality were necessary. It seemed an interesting twist that the moral clarity and pedagogical role came from the son rather than the father. As a father myself, I found it interesting, the idea of a man learning from his children."

Ledger sees the father/son disagreement over the war as an example of a classic generation gap. "While Gabriel is growing up, he hears all these fantastic war stories and it's all very, very heroic and glorious to him. His father had already been to war and become a famous warrior. And so he knew better, he knew how gory it could be. He's ashamed of who he has been in the past and what he has done. He doesn't want that side of Gabriel to come out at any point. He doesn't want to put his son in that situation. I think all parents and children go through that sort of thing at some point. To Gabriel, though, the idea of war is brave and adventurous and the right thing to do. Gabriel represents the new generation. He believes strongly in the new ideals of the new country. He's very proud and stubborn. And so he defies his father to go to war."

In the course of the film, Ledger's character matures from a boy to a man. His youthful patriotism collides with the bloody reality of war. The part required an actor who could convey both Gabriel's boyish impetuousness and the wisdom he attains as he matures. It also demanded an actor who could convincingly portray Gibson's screen son.

"Heath possesses qualities that link him to Mel and I think on screen it really comes off as a true father-and-son relationship, a very believable relationship," says Dean Devlin. "If you look at the early Mel Gibson movies, even when he was very young, he never seemed like a boy. There was something very manly about him, even at a young age. And I think that is true about Heath Ledger. He's twenty years old but he doesn't feel like a little boy, he feels like a man. I think they share that quality on screen. You feel that there is a weight to the things he has to say about the cause, about why they are fighting. It's very credible."

Gibson adds that he was very impressed with his co-star's concentration and earnest approach. "I really like the kid," he says simply. "He is far more mature than his age. He was very measured and very deliberate about his work. I remember what I was like when I was that age. God, I don't think I was capable of some of the more subtle things he's done. He was accurate and precise in what he did. I think he had fun as well, which is also important. He took it very seriously but he wasn't wound up about it. I think he's got a hell of a future. He's got the right sort of heart and spirit for the whole thing and he's just going to get better as he goes on."

Australian-born Ledger returns the compliment. "Mel is every Aussie's hero. It was an amazing opportunity to work with him. And I learned so much from him. A lot of it was unspoken – his professionalism, the way he treats people, how he presents himself in his work. He's extremely polite and genuine. He takes a real interest in everyone and it's the same when he's working. He gives so much, on and off screen."

A LETTER FROM GABRIEL:

I envy you, your youth and your distance from this cruel conflict of which I am a part … but I consider myself fortunate to be serving the cause of liberty and, though I fear death, each day in prayer… I reaffirm my willingness, if necessary, to give my life in its service. Pray for me, but, above all, pray for the cause. Your loving brother, Gabriel.

JASON ISAACS
—
COLONEL TAVINGTON

Jason Isaacs has co-starred in such films as Neil Jordan's critically acclaimed *The End of the Affair* and Michael Bay's *Armageddon*. In addition he has appeared in three Paul Anderson directed movies: *Event Horizon*, *Soldier*, with Kurt Russell and the British cult film *Shopping*. He appeared in *Dragonheart* with Dennis Quaid and made his feature film debut in *The Tall Guy* opposite Jeff Goldblum and Emma Thompson.

Born in Liverpool, England, he attended Bristol University, where in addition to studying law he also managed to direct and/or star in over twenty theater productions. After graduating he attended London's prestigious Central School of Speech and Drama, which led to a role as a series regular on the British TV show *Capitol City*.

Other British television credits include Lynda La Plante's controversial mini-series *Civvies*, opposite Peter O'Toole; *Taggart*, in which he played identical twins and a CBS mini series *The Last Don 2*. On stage he appeared in the Royal National Theatre production of Pulitzer Prize winning *Angels in America – Parts 1 & 2*.

Jason Isaacs, who plays Colonel Tavington, the leader of the elite British troops, the feared Green Dragoons and the film's personification of wickedness, is witty, affable, and self-deprecating in person and hopes the audience won't confuse the character with him. He says that the film's story of a family in turmoil was what first attracted him to the project. "The film has a real emotional heart to it and that's what first grabbed me, to be honest. When I got the script initially, I was unable to put it down and just sobbed at the story. Then, of course, I couldn't wait to get my teeth into Tavington, a character who was so evil. It really is a gift of a part," he says.

"I've played a number of bad guys, but Tavington was quite spectacularly evil and he was desperately unpopular. The character he is loosely based on was the most hated British soldier in the entire conflict. There was a phrase, 'Tarleton's Quarters.' To give Tarleton's Quarters to the enemy meant you killed them all, whether they surrendered or not. He was known as "Bloody Ban" and "The Butcher."

While researching Tarleton, Isaacs discovered some alarming similarities between himself and Bloody Ban. "I found that Tarleton was the third son of a merchant from Liverpool, which I also am. I thought that was a rather good omen. He studied law, which I did. And then he dropped out because he became addicted to gambling and whoring. I dropped out to go to drama school, which is not enormously different! And at that stage, obviously, our paths diverge. My theory is that he had a death wish. He just didn't care, which is why he won so many battles and why the enemy was so scared of him," he conjectures. "He became this fearless, kind of 'wanna die' warrior. He would ride for days and then plunge head-first into battle. He had no kind of technique and he wouldn't use military strategy. He would ride right through the middle, swinging his saber around. And he won because the enemy couldn't quite believe what was going on."

Colonel Tavington is a composite of several men including Lieutenant Colonel Banastre Tarleton.

Tarleton was born in Liverpool in 1754 and achieved his greatest reputation as an incomparable cavalry leader and lightning-fast attacker. He was also known for the violence and brutality he inflicted on his enemies. "Tarleton's Quarter" meant ordering his men to kill helpless Americans even after they had put down their weapons and waved the white flag. He continued his reign of terror until Cornwallis surrendered at Yorktown in 1781.

He returned to England and became a member of Parliament for Liverpool, putting behind him his violent past. He married the daughter of the Duke of Ancaster, was knighted by George IV and was made a full general in 1812. He died in 1833 at the age of seventy-eight.

TOM WILKINSON
—
LORD GENERAL CORNWALLIS

Tom Wilkinson recently appeared in Ang Lee's Civil War drama *Ride with the Devil*, opposite Tobey Maguire, Skeet Ulrich and Jewel. This was his second film with Lee; he played Mr. Dashwood in the director's 1995 film *Sense and Sensibility*, opposite Emma Thompson. One of the busiest actors in Britain and the United States, Wilkinson won praise and a BAFTA Award nomination for Best Supporting Actor for his portrayal of Fennyman in John Madden's Academy Award®-winning *Shakespeare in Love*. His performance as Gerald in Peter Cattaneo's Academy Award®-nominated comedy *The Full Monty* also won him a BAFTA Award nomination for Best Supporting Actor. Other film credits include *Rush Hour*, *The Governess*, *Wilde*, Gillian Armstrong's *Oscar and Lucinda*, Bille August's *Smilla's Sense of Snow*, Antonia Bird's *Priest*, Jim Sheridan's *In the Name of the Father* and David Hare's *Wetherby*. He recently completed *Chain of Fools* for Warner Bros.

A renowned stage actor in his native England, Wilkinson has performed at the Royal National Theatre, the Royal Shakespeare Company and The Oxford Playhouse. His stage work includes title roles in *Peer Gynt*, *Brand* and *Henry V*. He has also performed in such productions as *The Three Sisters*, *Uncle Vanya*, *Julius Caesar*, *Hamlet*, *The Merchant of Venice*, *The Crucible* and *As You Like It*. His U.K. television credits include *Prime Suspect* and *Martin Chuzzlewit*.

While regarded by American historians as the "villain" and the "vanquished," General Cornwallis was, at his best, a capable officer ultimately outmatched by French and American forces and overwhelmed by guerrilla tactics he was unable to counter. Ironically, he opposed the British policies that so antagonized his colonial brethren, but, good soldier and subject that he was, he dutifully fought against them for the Crown. After his defeat at Yorktown, he enjoyed a long and successful career in the service of his country as British Governor-General of India and Viceroy of Ireland.

Wilkinson's portrayal conveys the regal bearing, brisk demeanor, and patrician countenance of the aristocrat Cornwallis was. While Wilkinson studied Cornwallis a bit, he relied on the script to produce his interpretation of the man. "I've never been much of a research freak…Basically, what you have to do is play the character that is written. You can go and say, 'Well, actually, Cornwallis was this, that, and the other,' which might be in direct conflict to the script. What I read about Cornwallis was that he was dutiful, very competent, but not a genius soldier and an all-around good man. He went on to have a very long and

distinguished career in India and Ireland. He was part of that good tradition in the English aristocracy, which is still maintained to some extent, of public service, which he subscribed to very much. He wasn't a brilliant soldier but he did the best with what he had. He wasn't a Wellington, but he wasn't Napoleon. One of the things I did read was that he was a soldier

who did things by the book and he was faced with this militia that did not, so he didn't quite know how to deal with them. I think that's why these significant battles were lost in the south."

Wilkinson's first scene to be filmed was between Cornwallis and Tavington at the former's opulent headquarters. Tavington's brutal methods of warfare are supremely distasteful to the gentleman in Cornwallis, all the more so because they encapsulate Tavington's sole *raison d'être*: ambition.

"The British army at this time was very much a mirror of the kind of class system that existed in England. One of the areas of conflict between Tavington and Cornwallis is their difference in class. Although Tavington, I think, is well connected, he's not an aristocrat, so there is always that vague sense of disapproval that Cornwallis has for him. Of course, Tavington commits the very un-English sin of being fiercely ambitious," Wilkinson says.

In these first scenes, Jason Isaacs expected Wilkinson's Cornwallis to explode when faced with the consequences of Tavington's egregious violence. It has ignited and united the countryside, and now he has failed to capture Benjamin Martin, thus allowing Martin to put into effect an elaborate ruse that has completely bamboozled Cornwallis. Instead, Wilkinson undermined Isaacs' Tavington with an icy, contained contempt.

"'Bombastic' is not something that I think is part of Cornwallis' character. That is at odds with what I knew about him. He wasn't a blowhard. So I thought that he's not only got to be a guy who is up against it militarily, he's also got to be able to see the big game, which is the political consequences. He does realize that. He says, 'You have to remember that these are our brothers and when this conflict is over we're going to have to trade with them. They are our trade partners and we need them.' So I couldn't play him as a rabid, anti-American maniac. He had

to have an element of the diplomat in him as well. It wasn't like a war against the Nazis, a win-at-all-costs war where you demonize your opponent. It was simply a local conflict, which was very much the sort of thing that the British military had to deal with at this time – a local uprising that had to be gently put down and then things would carry on normally. So I felt that to make him a crazy man with smoke coming out of his ears would have been a wrong tactic, and boring as well. Fortunately, the script had little room for that kind of interpretation."

JOELY RICHARDSON
—
CHARLOTTE SELTON

Joely Richardson starred in the science fiction thriller *Event Horizon* and in the live-action version of *101 Dalmatians*. She recently completed the independent film *Under Heaven*. Other film credits include *Drowning by Numbers*, *Shining Through*, James L. Brooks's *I'll Do Anything*, the award-winning *Sister My Sister*, *Loch Ness*, *The Tribe* and Angela Pope's *The Hollow Reed*.

Born and raised in London, she attended the Royal Academy of Dramatic Art and made her film debut in David Hare's *Wetherby*, in which she played the part of her mother, Vanessa Redgrave, as a young girl. Upon graduation, she joined the Royal Shakespeare Company and starred in such productions as *A Midsummer Night's Dream*, *Macbeth* and *Worlds Apart*. Additional stage credits include *Beauty and the Beast* and *Steel Magnolias*. Her television work includes David Hare's *Heading Home* with Gary Oldman and a four-hour adaptation of D. H. Lawrence's *Lady Chatterley's Lover* directed by Ken Russell.

Joely Richardson plays Charlotte Selton, Martin's sister-in-law. Both she and Martin mourn the death of his wife, Elizabeth, but the connection between the two is deeper than their common grief.

"He is in mourning for his dead wife, which is something that Charlotte understands profoundly, because Elizabeth was her sister and because she also has experienced the death of her husband. So there is an element of shared grief, but through the years an unspoken spark has grown between them," Richardson explains. "It is an adult kind of affection and respect. It is not the young love of seventeen-year-olds, it is a seasoned love of people who have lived. It is very compassionate and unspoken."

Richardson says that the opportunity to participate in a movie of such historical scope attracted her, but "it was the personal stories, these fascinating characters with such interesting lives," that drew her to the script. "It was a terrifically good read that held my interest and imagination," she says simply. She describes Charlotte as "a lovely presence, very gentle and kind," but confesses that the part also came with another attraction, the kind that appeals to little girls of all ages.

"I watched *Gone with the Wind* as a child again and again. And for me there was that element of fantasy to *The Patriot*, although obviously it is not set in the same time period. On some level it was every fantasy I ever had as a child of dressing up. I think as little girls it's somehow imprinted on our minds, this idea of the romantic South, the shape that a corset will give you, the flowing skirts. When we shot at some of the plantations in South Carolina, there were people riding up on horses, and carriages coming back and forth, and I'd rush out in my Scarlett O'Hara kind of dress. It was a dream come true."

Richardson adds that in addition to experiencing the equivalent of a celluloid fairy tale, she looked forward to working with Roland Emmerich and Dean Devlin. She found them to be very "actor-friendly" filmmakers. "I liked the script enormously, but when I met Roland and Dean I really wanted the job. They're very open to their actors and to the crew. The first time I met them, I immediately felt welcomed and comfortable. Roland started taking me through all the storyboards, and I could see that he had an incredible eye for how it would look. And Dean, having been an actor, is very communicative and supportive. Both of them are very accessible, very funny, and cool."

The chance to work with Mel Gibson also had its attractions, although the thought of it was initially overwhelming. Her early anxieties evaporated, however, as soon as their scenes together began.

"I was really excited to work with Mel. He's famous for his sense of humor and tells jokes non-stop, which raises everyone's spirits. It also keeps your performance fresh, because it is: joke, joke, joke, action. And that's exhilarating. All of the sudden, on 'action,' he delivers this tremendous performance. It's been really great to watch him work and he was certainly very generous in the scenes that we had together. He's got an incredible, subtle range. He can have such mischief and sparkle in his eyes, but he also conveys such gravitas, such sadness. I'd sometimes look at him and think, 'I hope he's all right.' I think that's brilliant," she says.

LISA BRENNER

—

ANNE HOWARD

Lisa Brenner makes her film debut in *The Patriot*. She recently completed her second feature, *Roomies*, directed by Oliver Robins, a romantic comedy about two people looking for the perfect roommate. She began her career as Marguerite Cory on the classic daytime television drama *Another World*, appearing just before the show's demise, from 1995 to 1996. She also played Jenny on the MTV series *Undressed*, described as *The Real World* meets *Sex, Lies and Videotape*.

While Charlotte Selton is the film's quiet, nurturing, maternal figure, Anne Howard, played by Lisa Brenner, is her outspoken counterpart. Anne, who supports Gabriel Martin in his advocacy of the nascent country and its new ideals, is reminiscent of that feminine but strong-willed female paragon Abigail Adams, who advised her revolutionary husband John, "Remember the ladies, and be more generous and favorable to them than your ancestors. Do not put such unlimited power into the hands of the husbands…If particular care and attention is not paid to the ladies, we are determined to foment a rebellion and will not hold ourselves bound by any laws in which we have no voice or representation." Indeed, in preparation for her role, Brenner studied the famous future First Lady.

"Anne is a sixteen-year-old girl living in colonial times but she definitely has opinions about the war. If she could, she'd be fighting in it too. She's a 'pre-feminist.' She has passion and fire and ideals, like Gabriel, which I think, among other things, draws them together. There is a wonderful scene when Gabriel comes to the church to enlist some of his neighbors into the militia. At first, everyone shies away, but Anne stands up for him and talks everyone into it. When I first read it, I felt it was a little too much for that time, for a woman to say those kind of things. But when I read letters

from Abigail Adams to John Adams, she was as outspoken as Anne. She was his voice and his counsel but also his great love. So it wasn't as out of the ordinary as I originally thought."

Obviously, many of Brenner's scenes were with Heath Ledger, who occasionally greeted her with a happy, "Hello, wife!" *The Patriot* marks Brenner's film debut, so she appreciated working with such a supportive co-star. "Heath is just a wonderful actor and person – very charismatic, warm, fun and playful. I felt very comfortable with him. He started working on the film long before I did, and the way the schedule worked out, I came back and forth to set, so it could've been difficult, but he made it very easy. It wasn't hard work having to fall in love with Heath."

One of the couple's first scenes revolved around an eighteenth-century courting ritual that required Ledger to lie on a bed wrapped in a heavy cloth sheath. The idea was to allow the betrothed to socialize in a semi-unchaperoned way. Ledger amused Brenner and the crew between takes by overcoming his protective covering to unmistakably indicate his character's amorous intentions towards his bride-to-be. Lisa says, "There was a custom that if a boy was coming to call on a woman, the mother would place him in what was called a bundling bag and sew him into it so he could be next to her but nothing could happen physically. It was a very sweet scene, a lot of fun."

WOMEN IN THE AMERICAN REVOLUTION

At the start of the American Revolution, women seldom had independent status. When the war broke out, men were removed from the workplace and women became an integral part of the economy of the country. Although they had always contributed to the operation of farms and businesses, they now had to take full responsibility, which proved economically successful. As a result, issues of women's rights, education and their role in society were raised. When the war ended, a few states responded by modifying their laws on inheritance and property to permit women to inherit a share of estates and to control a limited amount of property after marriage. But for most women, there were only very gradual and diffuse improvements in their status. Rather than making women independent citizens with a political and civil standing equal to men's, the war gave fuller recognition only to mothers of republican citizens.

TCHEKY KARYO
—
MAJOR VILLENEUVE

Tcheky Karyo recently appeared in Luc Besson's *The Messenger*, his second picture for Besson, who also cast him in *La Femme Nikita*. Additional film credits include *Wing Commander*, Hugh Hudson's *My Life So Far*, *Addicted to Love*, directed by Griffin Dunne, *GoldenEye* and *Bad Boys*. His television credits include an episode of the HBO mini-series *From the Earth to the Moon*, directed by Tom Hanks, and *And the Band Played On*, also for HBO. Born in Turkey, he resides in Paris.

Tcheky Karyo based the character of the French officer Villeneuve partly on the young French fighter the Marquis de Lafayette. Lafayette volunteered for the American army and rose through the ranks to become Washington's protégé. With the help of his countrymen General Jean Rochambeau, the commander of the Gallic land forces in America and Admiral François de Grasse, the Marquis de Lafayette effectively trapped Cornwallis at Yorktown. Washington and his troops eventually joined the French and their combined forces of 16,000 men forced Cornwallis to surrender.

Karyo points out that France had ties to the New World, as well as a loathing for Britain and an enthusiasm for the ideas of independence and liberty that the American Revolution defined and defended. "Many French people settled in America as well as the English, so there was always a strong connection to France. The French were obviously attracted to the new lands – Villeneuve means 'new city' in French – but they were also intrigued by the new ideas. Lafayette became a symbol of the relationship between the French and the Americans, so I drew from him for Villeneuve."

The difference between Villeneuve and Lafayette, Karyo notes, is that Villeneuve's initial relationship with his American allies, particularly Benjamin Martin, is an uneasy one at best. "Villeneuve is a French officer, a major, from the Southern Light Foot Cavalry and he arrives to help Benjamin Martin's militia fight against the British Crown. But Martin was part of an assault during the French and Indian War, when the French and the colonists were on opposite sides. In that war, Villeneuve's family was massacred. So he is a man full of hate and revenge, just like Benjamin Martin. At first, those feelings divide them, but they learn to respect each other and realize that they have both lost their families to war."

Karyo describes Villeneuve as "elegant," in dress and sensibility; he's also an expert horseman. This is as true of Karyo as it is of his character, for the actor is a keen equestrian. On his days off, he generally honed his riding skills with the help of the film wranglers and some local ranchers he befriended.

MARQUIS DE LAFAYETTE AND THE ROLE OF THE FRENCH IN THE REVOLUTIONARY WAR

Many would find it surprising to learn that if the Americans had not joined with the French, they could not have won the Revolutionary War. French contributions to supplies and funds from 1776 to 1778 were invaluable and their naval and military support after 1778 was critical. Initially, aid from the French to the American cause was covert, but in 1778 they signed treaties of commerce and alliance, agreeing that neither the French nor the Americans would make peace with Britain until the independence of the United States was recognized. This put the French openly at war with Britain, but it also provided them with a defensive and commercial alliance should Britain attack.

One of the most revered and successful French officers of this time was the Marquis de Lafayette, who arrived in America and was made a major-general by the colonists. Among his contributions, he was able to get Cornwallis to retreat across Virginia, entrapping him at Yorktown. He was then joined by his close friend, General George Washington, and a French naval fleet. The joint siege led to the surrender of Cornwallis and the defeat of the British. For his efforts, Lafayette was declared "the hero of two worlds," and when he returned to France in 1782 he was promoted to maréchal de camp (brigadier-general). In 1784 he became a citizen of the United States. He died in Paris in 1834 at the age of seventy-seven.

CHRIS COOPER
—
COLONEL BURWELL

Chris Cooper recently stunned critics and audiences with his mesmerizing portrayal of a conflicted, autocratic ex-Marine in Sam Mendes' *American Beauty*, opposite Kevin Spacey and Annette Bening. In 1999 he also starred as the father of an amateur rocket enthusiast in the acclaimed coming-of-age drama *October Sky*. Earlier he had earned praise, as well as a Best Actor nomination from the 1997 Independent Spirit Awards, for his work in John Sayles' *Lone Star*. He made his film debut nearly a decade before that in Sayles' *Matewan*. He stars in the forthcoming film from the Farrelly brothers, *Me, Myself and Irene*, opposite Jim Carrey. His previous movies include Robert Redford's *The Horse Whisperer*, *Great Expectations*, *A Time to Kill*, *Money Train*, *This Boy's Life*, *Guilty by Suspicion* and *City of Hope*.

As Colonel Burwell, Chris Cooper personified a different kind of elegance from Villeneuve's. A reserved, dignified man, he embodied the quiet resolve of the soldier/statesman.

"We were excited to land Chris Cooper, who was coming off two amazing performances in *October Sky* and *American Beauty*. He plays Martin's oldest friend, who he fought with in the previous war, and they have to communicate so much of this past in an unspoken way, between the lines, in terms of their friendship and what they mean to each other. It took an actor as fine as Chris to go toe-to-toe with Mel and to convey a wealth of history that's just based on a look and the manner in which they deal with each other," Devlin says.

Cooper explains: "[As] the one character who has gone through the previous battles in the French and Indian War with him, Burwell was somebody who understood Martin's horror of war…but he had also seen his bravery, having fought side by side with him, and is the one person who can appeal to his sense of honor and duty, because of their shared past."

Cooper acknowledges that Burwell is loosely based on Colonel "Lighthorse" Harry Lee, but the

filmmakers later fictionalized the character, partly because Lee was around nineteen when he fought in the Revolution. This was one of the little historical facts that Cooper learned in the course of the film, and he confesses that before he began *The Patriot*, he knew little about the Revolutionary War. "I live in Massachusetts, so it was a little embarrassing to realize I knew so little about my history. I read a number of books in preparation, but I knew we'd be in good hands, in terms of authenticity, when I heard that the Smithsonian was involved. Of course, having Roland as a director was also a good thing, and it doesn't hurt to work with Mel Gibson."

Cooper, whose character leads the Continental Army alongside Martin's militia in the decisive Battle of Cowpens, adds that shooting on location and charging into the fray with hundreds of extras, as cannons, mortars and musket fire exploded around him, was an invaluable experience. "I just think it was simply essential, a huge help. To look over at this group of militia who are the ragtag group of Patriots, to see the whole group assembled with a line of the Blue Coats, going into battle over the ridge, facing a line of British, it was very emotional. It really helped set the mood," he says.

PART III

—

BRINGING
THE PATRIOT
TO LIFE

THE SMITHSONIAN JOINS THE TEAM

The creators of *The Patriot* had set themselves the difficult task of bringing history to life and to do this they turned for help to the Smithsonian Institution. Associate producer Dionne McNeff, who served as the chief liaison to the Smithsonian, explains that one of the challenges of the film was achieving "subtle accuracy". "The art department, costume, hair and make-up people do their jobs so well, you don't necessarily notice because everything looks perfectly believable. The Smithsonian was very helpful in this regard."

The Smithsonian advisors did more than just make sure the historical details were accurate, as Stephen Lubar, Chairman of the Division of Historical Technology, explains. "Its most important role was helping the filmmakers think about a higher kind of historical accuracy. Smithsonian advisors helped to make sure the film reflected the culture of the time and captured some of the complexity of political and social issues."

The Smithsonian is the largest museum, research and education complex in the world, so it's no wonder the filmmakers would want to use its resources. But the Smithsonian had its own reasons for creating an alliance. Lee Woodman, the executive producer of Smithsonian Entertainment, a division of Smithsonian Business Ventures, explains, "For some years now we've been looking for ways for the Smithsonian to get its resources out to a wider audience. To this end, film makes a lot of sense. Many people learn about history through film. *The Patriot* was a perfect project for us to work on, not only because it's about the Revolutionary War but because we also really loved the approach the producers were taking toward the film. They had such an interest in history, and such an interest in getting the details right. I think the goal for both of us was to establish the true feeling of the period."

Rex Ellis, Chairman of the Cultural Division at the National Museum of History, adds, "The producers and Roland didn't want to get so caught up in the minutiae of the Revolutionary War that they sacrificed the story, but they wanted to be responsible to the history that was there. That balance of trying to tell a good story and trying to tell a credible story impressed the Smithsonian."

In the summer of 1999, a group including producer Dean Devlin, executive producer Bill Fay, and the production, costume, and prop designers visited the Smithsonian for a behind-the-scenes look at, among other things, the Armed Forces, Domestic Life, and Cultural History collections. One of the highlights of the tour was coming face to face with George Washington's battle sword. They also met consultants who were able to give the designers' general knowledge specific focus.

As Smithsonian costume specialist Shelly Foote says, "For most costume designers, seeing the real thing is quite different than seeing it in books. When you see them in living color, you can see the sheen of the fabrics; you can actually see the shape of the fabrics, how they drape."

Shelly Foote, Smithsonian Institution Costume Specialist

Academy Award®-winning costume designer Deborah L. Scott appreciated the input and having access to their vast collections. "It was really important to see some of the actual garments from the period. In my designs and the way I work, I'm very detail-oriented, so it was incredibly helpful to see real shirts, real uniforms – to see the way things were stitched and made and cut – because it was very, very different from the clothes we wear today."

Sarah Rittgers, a specialist in the Armed Forces collection, consulted with prop-master Doug Harlocker on several weapons, including the firearms used by the Continentals and the British, as well as the type of weapon that Mel Gibson's character could have carried. Rittgers says that she "pulled out a variety of weapons…and it helped them to look at authentic pieces so that they could manufacture their own reproductions." Beyond the types of weapons, Rittgers recalls, "One of the things we talked about at great length with *The Patriot* film crew was the whole process of what you have to do to get your musket or rifle ready in order to shoot, and then the process of the actual loading and firing."

Production designer Kirk M. Petruccelli, set decorator Victor Zolfo, and art director Barry Chusid began collaborating with the Smithsonian early on. "I met with each of the specialists to create the eighteenth-century look," Petruccelli explains. "This was a great opportunity to go in and really take a good hard look in great detail at every element and verify that we were going in the right direction. Working with the Smithsonian helped us to be as accurate to the time as possible." According to Zolfo, "They were incredible about providing materials that we couldn't find elsewhere. We kept coming up with really specific questions – lighting questions, for example. They told us that it was just candles at this point, so we realized that we were restricted and built many reflective sconces and multi-armed candleholders."

One of the areas where the Smithsonian was most influential was in the design of the Gullah village, the sanctuary for Benjamin Martin's family that is home to slave and freed African-Americans. According to director Emmerich, the Gullah "was originally up in the mountains and then Rex Ellis from the Smithsonian told us that the only villages of this kind were in these marshes and swamps."

McNeff explains, "The portrayal of African-Americans in the script was broadened by their insight. What a slave or freedman would have run away to do, where he would have gone, and what it would have looked like was information we got from the Smithsonian." According to Ellis, "In these kinds of scenes, you're constantly seeing blacks in the fields working, but very seldom do we see their lives outside of their service to whites. Here we show a community, a culture, that is in some way vibrant in and of itself." Screenwriter Rodat recalls how Ellis suggested that "when Martin's family is in jeopardy, they should hide at one of the Gullah villages. We actually rewrote it that way, which led to a number of dramatic elements."

The Smithsonian's suggestions covered a wide range of topics, occasionally relating to far more subtle elements, like language. McNeff recalls that they "suggested that General Cornwallis's manservant would never address him as 'sir', it would always be 'm'lord'. A nice little detail that people might not notice."

Summing up the help that the crew of *The Patriot* received from them, Devlin remarked, "Having the Smithsonian participate with us was like having a big brother on set who could nudge you and say, 'You've gone too far,' or 'You're missing something that would be interesting.'"

Right: Prop-Master Doug Harlocker and Costume Designer Deborah L. Scott inspect the Smithsonian Institution's gun collection

Above: Rex Ellis, Chairman of the Cultural Division of the National Museum of History, with Mel Gibson

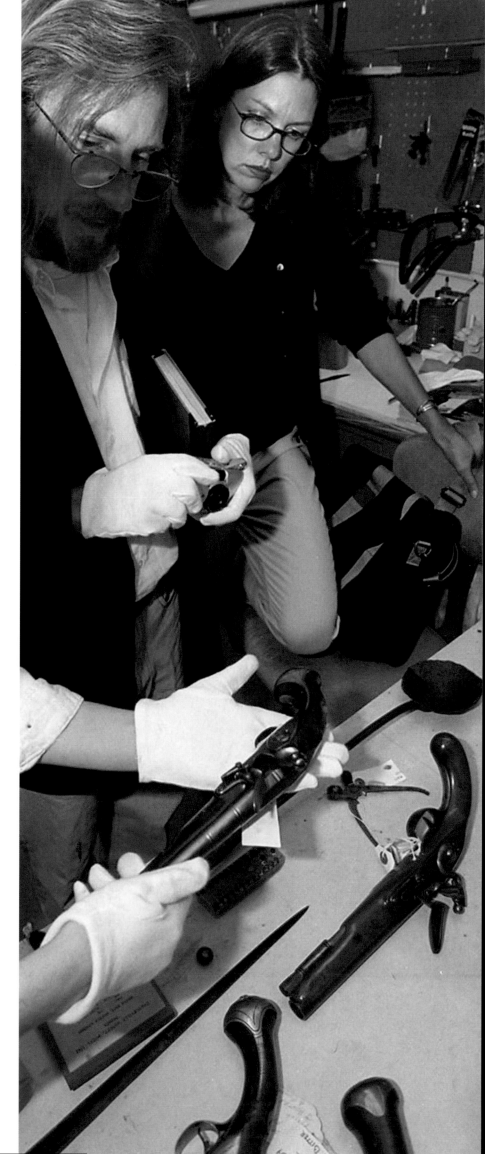

TAVINGTON:
My Lord, they're not like regulars. We can't find them and we don't know when or where they're going to strike.

CORNWALLIS:
Colonel, they're militia! Farmers with pitchforks!

TAVINGTON:
They're more than that, My Lord. Made so by their commander, this "Ghost".

COSTUMES
AND COLOR

Academy Award®-winning costume designer Deborah L. Scott worked closely with production designer Kirk M. Petruccelli and director Roland Emmerich. She employed a similar color progression to Petruccelli and used it to help define the characters.

The use of color in the film was metaphoric, with certain colors relating to wealth, power, or the lack thereof. Color was also used to represent the different periods and situations in the film. The beginning of the film is a very optimistic time for the colonial people so there was an abundance of warm tones and bright colors. As the British had not yet begun to dominate the story, they are seen as very understated. There was a sense of purity that prevailed at this point. However, once the British become a force, so do their hues, full of bold tones and primary colors. In response to the growing strength and presence of the British, the colonial colors became more muted, almost weak which suggested their struggle and near defeat.

In addition to the color progression, Scott did screen tests of various shades of red, blue and green in order to select the actual colors that would work best on film. As she explains, "Film stocks render color differently in different light, so we tested ten to fifteen similar shades of these three colors because they really change on film from what your eye sees. For example, we were looking for that perfect shade of navy blue that could go dark, but you knew it was blue." Adding to the challenge, they were short on prep time and the volume of material available, so "You couldn't just go to the fabric store, not with the quantities we needed."

Once the colors had been tested and determined, it was time to get to work on creating the look of each character. Scott explains, "Different characters go through different changes, depending on where they are at in the movie, but basically each character is a color palette unto themselves. For instance, Benjamin Martin has seven children and with that many, it's hard to keep them all separated in your mind. Visually, their personal colors provide a subtle little clue. One wears more green, another more gray, another more beige, another more golden. Gabriel starts off the movie as a strapping young man who is still a child and his style changes dramatically from there to when he puts on his uniform, when he decides to join the war, two years later."

She adds that as Gabriel becomes a man and endures hardship and war, his garb also incrementally begins to reflect his father's. "Mel's character is really represented strongly in his clothes: he wears a lot of black. Black has a lot of different meanings. It connotes maturity, strength, his position as a father and the head of his family. Next to him, Gabriel's colors are more muted and pale, the tones less saturated.

By the end of the movie, as they become closer, as the Benjamin Martin character softens and Gabriel becomes more

adult and confident, their wardrobe is more closely related."

Although Gibson's costumes were limited, they were crucial. "It was really important to portray Benjamin Martin heroically, as very strong and very focused. He really only had about six different kinds of outfits, mostly because when he finally goes off with the militia, it would be almost impossible for him to find too many different things to wear. So it was a matter of using the same garments over and over in different ways, in different situations," Scott says.

The women's costumes also reflected their characters. Scott assigned blues and greens to the feisty Anne Howard – no pink, frilly stuff for her, as exemplified by her sea-green silk wedding dress.

The gentle Charlotte, however, wore more classically feminine colors, including rosy tones and creams.

In addition to representing the characters, the women's wardrobes consciously evoked the society of the period.

According to Scott, "The women in the film are really the best place to show instantly where you are in the scope of time, because women's fashions change so quickly. They provided the opportunity to show the beauty and the time and place of the period.

"Charlotte, played by Joely Richardson, is the most wealthy, city-oriented person in the film, and she goes through a tremendous change, not only physically but also emotionally through what happens to her in the story. And it's really important to me as a costume designer to show those kinds of changes through people's clothing. She starts off in a very soft sort of color palette, very fancily dressed, with an exaggerated silhouette, and then slowly she changes. She goes to her house in the country and she becomes a little less structured, and her dress then becomes a little richer in hue. When the family must escape to the freed slave territory, when she essentially abandons her old life, she becomes much freer as a person, she's not so covered up. It's an interesting palette, an intriguing journey of a person.

"As for Lisa Brenner's Anne Howard, she is a middle-class girl of the time. She often wears the color light blue. A lot of that had to do with her environment and a lot of that had to do with the softness of the color and the identification of the character. But she also comes from a family that has access to basic fabrics but not to fine ones."

Obviously certain historical details affected Scott's color palette and costume choices. The British were not called Redcoats for nothing. "The British and Continental armies were in colors of red, white, and blue. Very striking, strong tones, especially red. Next to the red of the movie, anything else really pales by comparison. The military uniforms are as historically based as possible.

"I also researched a lot of what was the fashion of the eighteenth century. The colonies were very European in nature at that point. All their trade was with Europe, so they had access to fabric that you wouldn't normally think they would have. In fact, in those years cotton was a rarity. Silk was more the material of choice, because there was a ban on cotton in England. Most of the styles that we used were English-based, and because there were no photographs, we looked to painters. John Singleton Copley and Gainsborough were the artists I studied very closely. I then coordinated with production design, especially in terms of the family, to determine the level at which they lived and the kind of clothes they would wear," Scott says.

She had to outfit not only the principal cast but also, quite literally, an army of extras. She reckons her department supplied roughly 1200 uniforms to the film. "We had a tremendous amount of background in this film, including a great deal of information supplied by the Smithsonian. The most important players in terms of the story, of course, were the soldiers. None of their uniforms really existed in any costume houses, so we had to start from scratch. And we wanted it to be very obvious about the two sides, because in reality there was a lot more mixing of colors. It's important visually to get a very strong sense of who is who on the battlefield, and that was one of the things Roland really wanted to see. In his mind's eye, in those battles, particularly the first Battle of Camden, where we had soldiers spread across the field, it was crucial to see red and blue very strongly coming together in a clash."

As a result, the costumes for the Green Dragoons, an actual sector of the British army, underwent serious modifications. As Scott explains, "It was really important that they be dashing and

heroic, but it was also important that we changed their uniforms to be mostly red and a little green so that immediately you knew they were British."

Ultimately, Scott says, "We had to manufacturer thousands of garments, and in our biggest scene we ended up dressing 800 or 900 soldiers. On top of that we outfitted about 200 militia, who were dressed in civilian-type wear."

A period film of this size was an undertaking that required a global effort. According to Scott, "We set up our shop and that included twenty people who just worked on building, aging, dyeing and manufacturing hats, jewelry and shoes because they're not available to rent. The clothes available for rental came from all over, not only the United States but also London, Paris, Vienna and Rome."

Eventually it all came together. "The moment the actor puts the costume on is when it comes alive, and seeing them walk around in something that you've designed is when you know you've really succeeded, and it feels great."

FACTS AND FIGURES

The costumes were rented from three English, eight Italian, one French, one Austrian and at least eight American costume houses.

The costume department manufactured approximately 1200 military uniforms for the film.

Each uniform consists of approximately nine pieces: coat, shirt, vest, hat, neckstock, breech, stockings, gators, shoes. All of these nine pieces arrived new and had to be "aged" by textile artists to look as though the soldiers had worn them for several months.

All uniforms were historically accurate except the Green Dragoons' which were original designs created for the movie based on factual information.

22,100 extras in total were dressed throughout the entire production

The costume department ordered 83,900 military buttons made with historic detail in three different sizes for uniforms. The buttons for British uniforms had to be additionally brass-plated.

The costume department ordered approximately 3000 pairs of stockings for extras on the film.

Mel Gibson had ten identical complete costumes for his fight sequence with Tavinington. Tavington had six complete identical costumes for the same sequence.

The costume department traveled with ladies' and mens' made-to-order tailor shops: two milliners, four textile agers and dyers, three supervisors, one assistant designer and innumerable costumers as well as the costume designer.

The main "in-house" laundry had eight washers and eight dryers as well as one 55-pound industrial washer and one 75-pound industrial dryer. It often had to turn around between 500 and 700 shirts and 500 and 700 pairs of stockings in less than twelve hours.

475 pounds of dry pigment (also known as fuller's earth) were used for aging clothes.

The costume department went through 12 gallons of fake blood . This did not not include fake blood used by make-up, special effects or props.

WEAPONS AND PROPS

Prop-master Doug Harlocker had the daunting task of propping not just the principal actors but hundreds of soldiers and the various sets and locations. These props, which required exceptional care and detail, included vintage cutlery, plates and bowls; children's playthings and school gear, ranging from chalkboards and toy soldiers to a replica vintage doll made by a specialist; General Cornwallis' elegant possessions, such as silver candelabra, silver-topped decanters and his snuff box, spyglasses, compass and sextant; all the odd accoutrements carried by soldiers, from their leather backpacks to the militia's pouches and powderhorns; miscellaneous period neccessities, such as quill pens and "pounce boxes," from which people shook powder over their inky signatures on parchment to dry them. Of course, a movie set against the backdrop of war required many weapons, from sabers, daggers and bayonets to pistols and rifles…lots of rifles.

"The Smithsonian was a fantastic resource, because they have the best of everything. We went through the gun room and found great examples of what existed then," recalls Harlocker. "We had about 290 rifles on the prop truck at any given time. We also had rifles and guns specially made for Mel's character, by Frank House. Frank is based in Tennessee and is the premiere gun maker in America."

As House explains, "Doug Harlocker contacted me and we discussed what kind of rifle the character would have been carrying. He was a fairly prosperous farmer, out of the Tidewater South Carolina area. There was one very well-documented rifle that was captured at the Battle of Buford's Mill, the John Thomas rifle. We took some of the influence from that gun. It also shows a lot of English influence because of the Tidewater association with England. We made a rifle that would probably have been built in the late 1770s and used as civilian-type rifle. A person like Benjamin Martin might have a gun like this because it was quite a show of prosperity to own a very nice rifle. Basically, they only had so many ways to demonstrate their wealth: good horses, good rifles and good farms. A man's primary status symbol in the eighteenth century was his rifle."

Of course, Gibson had to learn how to handle his weapons, from muskets to tomahawks, with the ease and dexterity of a

former guerrilla fighter. In particular, he had to master the fine and very intricate art of speed-loading. It was especially important for Mel to learn from the experts, because, according to Harlocker, "There's very specific parts of the movie where he's going to kill twenty-five people and it's just him and a couple of guys."

Enter Mark Barron, who trained Daniel Day-Lewis for *The Last of the Mohicans*. The combination of Barron and House gave Gibson the most well-rounded training, including running and speed-loading at the same time – not an easy task, considering the guns were six feet long.

"Speed-loading means taking little lead balls packed into a hunk of wood, held with the cloth and pig grease or tallow already on them. These are injected with a ram rod down the barrel of a rifle, which has already had fifty grains of black powder in it. You've got to ram it, take it back out, and turn it over, and then you've got to prime the pan, which is where the term 'flash in the pan' comes from, which feeds into a hole and ignites the powder inside the barrel and propels the ball out. But it's a very fiddly deal. It was a long, drawn-out process. It takes about twenty seconds between shots and that's if you're going flat out, like a running rabbit, provided you don't make any mistakes. It's quite an experience," Barron says.

Benjamin Martin was also given a tomahawk, which Harlocker created from a hybrid of seven different designs because, he says, "I wanted to make it individual." The work itself was done by two separate experts. Renowned sword and knife maker Tony Swanton hand-forged the blade and hand-engraved it, while premiere furniture maker and carpenter Jim Betts made the handle.

"The tomahawk includes commemorative engraving which would have been a symbol of prior conflict, in this case the French and Indian War," Harlocker explains.

All the weapons were obviously designed to look realistic for the battle and fighting scenes, so it was an added challenge to create collapsible swords and bayonets. These would retract on impact so that the impaling looked natural. No real ammunition was used during production.

Not everyone in the film would die instantly, so Harlocker had to provide historically accurate medical supplies for the production as well. These included amputation and cranial bone saws, as well as wooden boxes for portable surgery implements. The bone saws were ebony-handled with hand-forged steel and hand-made blades.

According to Harlocker, "All of these items were made

especially for the film because they do not exist, except in a museum like the Smithsonian. We couldn't find anything in books of bone saws and amputation saws, but the Smithsonian had perfect examples of complete kits, with beautifully detailed wooden cases and every imaginable instrument intact."

Harlocker paid just as much attention to detail when creating props that established the home life of the characters. Among them, he commissioned a baker who was an expert in eighteenth-century recipes to create breads and pies for the production.

One of the best examples of the lengths that Harlocker's team went to in order to make a beautiful, historically accurate prop was the doll that Martin's youngest daughter, Susan, carries. Designed by Hanna Hyland, the foremost period-doll maker, Harlocker describes it as "hand-made, with hand-carved wooden hands, arms, feet, and face, hand-embroidery on the dress, which was made from cloth of the period, and hand-painted. It also featured hand-woven genuine hair in the style of the period. The detail is exactly the way it would have been for an upper-class woman like Charlotte."

Some of the props that Harlocker created weren't as rooted in tradition, including the bundling bag that Gabriel is sewn into when he calls on Anne. It was thought to be a tradition to allow young men who traveled a great distance to court a young lady to stay the night like this without any risk of impropriety. But, according to Harlocker, "No research exists to authenticate the bundling bag's existence, so we based it on what we believed it to be. Linen was the fabric of the time, so we took a hard linen, lined it, and sewed it up with waxed string which prevented it from rotting."

Harlocker sums up his experience by saying, "This period is more of a challenge because, unlike the nineteenth century, there is not a lot of material that is already in existence or that has already been re-created, so this production required a lot of manufacturing. The challenge was exciting and well worth it."

TAVINGTON:

This man has the loyalty of many people. They protect him, his location, his family, the families of his men. To capture him would entail the use of tactics that are…what was the word you used…brutal?

SETS AND LOCATIONS

The Patriot used various locations throughout northern South Carolina, in and around a small community called Rock Hill, before ending the film in the graceful city of Charleston, North Carolina. While the filmmakers originally scouted such far-flung places as Canada, Ireland and New Zealand, the Carolinas proved to be the most advantageous shooting locale for several reasons.

"A number of factors go into choosing certain main locations. Price is certainly one consideration and the look is the other main one. We knew we needed huge, unspoiled distances for these enormous eighteenth-century battle scenes," explains executive producer Bill Fay. "On our first trip to the Carolinas we saw some interesting places, although it took several scouts to discover them. Beyond that, there were so many other reasons why we should be shooting in the Carolinas. Obviously, the story takes place there and the fact that it is an American story made us feel that we should try to keep it in the United States. Another big factor for us was that all period props, wardrobe and set dressing were available in the South. Also, the quality of the extras…I'm not sure why but you just see some amazing faces in the South."

Pembroke and the Martin Plantation

The first scenes to be shot were at the Martin plantation, on 280 acres of land that collectively became known as Fresh Water and across a small creek, the village of Pembroke. The route leading to the location was called Fishing Creek Presbyterian Road, so named for Reverend John Simpson's Fishing Creek Presbyterian Church. The British Captain Christian Huck specifically targeted Reverend Simpson, torching his home. *The Patriot*'s British forces repeated that conflagration twice on this property, first torching the Martins' house and then the church in the neighboring town of Pembroke. Of course, these blazes were set with fire trucks and extinguishers nearby.

Pembroke and the Martin homestead, with its adjacent barn/workroom, its crops, and even its gates, did not exist prior to filming. It fell to production designer Kirk M. Petruccelli, art director Barry Chusid, construction coordinator Bob Blackburn and set decorator Victor Zolfo to realize Roland Emmerich's vision of these and the rest of the film's sets. Emmerich is routinely described as a "visual director," and now they have actual proof.

"We sat down with Roland and discussed the locations and he sketched out his ideas for the sets on parchment as we talked. So we had a series of drawings to work from after the meeting, which was very helpful," Chusid says.

Petruccelli explains that all the sets were based on history and the characters who inhabited them. He even had to build his own eighteenth-century town, the village of Pembroke. "In the

town of Pembroke, we built the church first, at the highest point on the hilltop, as the settlers probably would have. From that we built down. Then we asked what was the basis of the town? There would be agriculture, so one of the buildings sells goods for farming. There was a blacksmith's and place that sold tack, because the horse was the main form of transportation at that time. Then there would be people who began living in the town, so certain other types of business would arise, such as a tavern. We examined the social, political and religious needs of the town and it sprang from that."

Martin's house was a tricky build, as it had to contain interior sets, such as bedrooms, Martin's study, the parlor and the kitchen, as well as an exterior porch, but it also had to burn quickly and realistically when "the British" rode in and torched it. The construction crew assembled an ingenious half-hollow house, building the minimum requisite sets against a skeleton of scaffolding and wooden beams. Some of the surrounding greenery was as fake as the house. While real tobacco and millet grew in the fields, watered by five wells drilled by the production, faux Spanish moss hung from the trees, some of which grew only silk leaves. In the distance, the special effects team pumped smoke through a lengthy rubber tube perforated with holes along the top, all of which conspired to create morning and evening "mist" for certain scenes.

While the façade may have been artificial, the details were as authentic as possible. Martin's house, a sturdy, unpretentious building with high ceilings and long corridors, gray-green walls, dark wooden furniture, light fixtures holding gold tapers and an aged brick fireplace in one room and a marble one in another, was the picture of colonial, masculine taste. Yet there were small signs that a woman's touch had once graced the house too.

This, says set decorator Victor Zolfo, was the result of director Roland Emmerich and production designer Kirk M. Petruccelli's interest in creating character-reflective settings. "It all starts with Roland, always. Roland was with us through every step of the design process in Los Angeles. We approached Roland and said, for example, 'How much of [Benjamin Martin's deceased wife] Elizabeth do we want to see in his house?' The answer was that there should be elements revealing that there was a tremendous amount of fondness and memory of Elizabeth in the house, but that it really has become Martin's house. We placed a piece of embroidery in the living room and there were some Merrymen plates along the fireplace that were probably wedding gifts. We tried to display a few special things in the house which signified their union and their wedding and were keepsakes. There was not a hugely feminine influence in the house, just a few accents. We wanted it to look like he was an important person, someone the community respects and looks up to, but at the same time that he has created this idyllic life for himself and his kids."

Like several other departments, Chusid, Zolfo and their

crews began their research with the Smithsonian. This led them to several other highly regarded organizations that specialize in the period and the region, and slowly an array of experts and craftsmen emerged.

Zolfo explains, "We just started this whole network that began with the Smithsonian, with the Williamsburg Foundation and with Old Salem and the Museum of Early Southern Decorative Arts. They would put us in touch with the crafts-people who devote their lives to making these kinds of things – basket weavers and calligraphers and potters and blacksmiths and tinsmiths. A lot of times, there were things like the iron that we built exactly the same way they would've in the eighteenth century. The blacksmiths who worked with us are schooled in period smithing and that's their passion, it's what they want to do. The tinsmiths who re-created a lot of our tin lanterns and sconces…one was a fourth-generation tinsmith who does museum work. We were very fortunate. We approached these people, many of whom had never done this type of thing for a film before. They were very excited about it and a lot of them actually traveled a great distance to see the sets once they were up. It was really wonderful to do it that way. We rented from antique stores and we purchased things, but a lot of times it was easier to have craftspeople manufacture things we wanted themselves."

Benjamin Martin's house highlighted the talents of these special artisans, particularly the kitchen, with its crockery and iron labyrinth of cooking utensils. "We had a lot of fun with all the iron in Martin's house, especially in the kitchen. The kitchen was this fabulous extension of every kitchen we'd seen in Williamsburg and in all of our research. We had things going on in that kitchen that probably would've made an eighteenth-century Martha Stewart jealous. The pottery was all made for us by this wonderful potter named Michelle Ericson up in Yorktown. She actually does a lot of the pottery for Williamsburg and a lot of the village restorations on the East Coast. She re-created redware and slipware and pots and mugs. Just about everything in the set was made for it."

Of course, there were practical reasons for manufacturing the goods in Martin's house. "When we were in big sets like Martin's house for a long time, we figured it would be safer to have things created. Plus, we never knew what was going to burn. It seemed like there were so many sets in the movie that were going to catch on fire at some point that we figured we'd better just make

things. Amazingly, we made out pretty well, there wasn't much damage," Zolfo says.

There were some authentic pieces in the film, mostly but not exclusively in Cornwallis' headquarters. "Just on a whim, we called the Wrights-Ferry Museum and told the curators that we'd seen this wonderful silk-on-silk embroidery, was there any way we could use it? They were very excited about it and they loaned it to us. It was originally in Benjamin's house, but we didn't see it, so we moved it to Anne Howard's house. That happened a lot on this movie. We would create something that we really wanted to feature and then for some reason, the way the scene was blocked [sketched out], we didn't see it, so we just moved it somewhere else where it would be appropriate. If we built something for Cornwallis, eventually it was somewhere that Cornwallis was."

Lighting, specifically candlelight, also became a collaboration between the art department and the camera, grip and electric crews. The cucalorus, a large square riddled with oval cutouts, was an ubiquitous presence on the set. Set in front of a light and gel, it helped mimic firelight. Even the type of candle was scrutinized by director of photography, Caleb Deschanel.

"Caleb really wanted to do the entire movie with candlelight. We re-created in prep something like two dozen different kinds of candles, with two- and three-braided wicks and all kinds of beeswax to try to figure out what gave the best light," Zolfo recalls. "Caleb tested the whole range of colors and he and Kirk, working with the kind of [film stock] that they were using, arrived with what would work inside, which then dictated to me where I could go with the fabrics and colors. Caleb said, 'If you're going to go with a damask and this kind of gold, it has to be a more yellow gold, as opposed to a cooler one.' Stuff like that. It was an enormous help. It's funny, because when you do a contemporary film the director of photography wants as many fixtures and practicals [actual light sources used as props] as you can put in the room so that there are always light sources, and it wasn't any different with candles. It was a constant challenge to figure out how to put candles in the rooms. I think we had more candles in this movie than they had in the entire eighteenth century."

Cornwallis' Headquarters

The Swamp

Perhaps the most colorful set of the movie is the interior of General Cornwallis' headquarters, an elegant turquoise drawing room with gold chandeliers and dark, sophisticated Chippendale furniture. This set, Petruccelli explains, marks the British at the peak of their power. The interior, which Petruccelli says was inspired by Cornwallis' personality, was built in a sprawling fortress known as Fort Carolina, which was based on the house of a colonial officer.

"Fort Carolina was based on 'Lighthorse,' Harry Lee's original structure called Stratford Hall, a beautiful Virginian mansion. We wanted to go a little bit more up country, to get him away from the lower South Carolina architecture, and we also wanted a very stark, stoic, linear structure. We used Stratford Hall because of the style and magnitude of it and because of when it was built. This was in the early 1700s and it was a massive, H-patterned house. The interior parlor had to reflect Cornwallis' character: it had to be bigger than words, flamboyant yet simple, opulent and beautiful, the kind of place that Cornwallis would walk into and say, 'I like this house. It's mine.' Then we fortified it, as the British would have done to captured plantation houses. That meant a lot of earth and tree work, building fence lines, 600 feet of 12- to 18-foot timbers, a wall with gallows, a jail cell system, a tent encampment, all on an immense scale," Petruccelli says. "There were some genuine period pieces in the Cornwallis set, some very valuable statuary…There was a painting that was valued at well over $500,000. It was a painting of the first Governor of Georgia over the mantel and we never took our eyes off of it."

The conflict in which Martin's militia, hiding in the swamps, overtakes a British unit in the quintessential surprise attack took place in a man-made marsh near Charleston. The swamp, known as Cypress Gardens, is a tourist destination created in the late 1920s.

Cypress Gardens was originally part of Dean Hall, one of the Cooper River's most important rice plantations which flourished from the eighteenth century until the Civil War. It also happened to be near a train route and in the flight path of a nearby airport. The consequent traffic provided an ongoing challenge for sound mixer Lee Orloff. Near the end of the film, second assistant Lars Winther took to pinning train schedules to the sound board and the video monitors.

Since it was a fabricated swamp, the production was able to drain its tannic waters to ascertain how safe it was to send cameras, horses and personnel across and also where to position all the equipment and actors. Ultimately, the production lowered the water table eight feet, built an island encampment that featured the "ruins" of an old Spanish mission and planted an eerie garden of crosses and headstones nearby, where the mission's former inhabitants rested for eternity.

The crew also constructed a long, raised platform sturdy enough to support a dolly track, the dolly and camera and its operators. This allowed Emmerich to film a wide shot that followed Martin's men as they rose from behind trees in the swamp to fire at the British as they traveled down a skinny patch of land. A thick layer of mist, courtesy of the special effects department, added a spooky feel to the scene, and most of the

The Gullah Maroon

In stark contrast to this refined and decadent setting was the freed slave territory, shot at Botany Bay Plantation on Edisto Beach. This plantation was, in fact, a 5000-acre wildlife preserve. Thatched huts, African-style woven baskets and blankets dotted a thin stretch of beach that represented the oasis to which the Martin family escape. Thousands of seashells crunched beneath the cast and crew's feet as they scrambled around the seashore, trying to make the most of the limited daylight left in the winter months. Although the production shorthand for this location was "the Gullah Maroon," Gullah, in fact, is a language based on English and various West African dialects spoken on the Sea Islands of South Carolina.

For Beatrice Bush, who played Abigale, Benjamin Martin's freed slave who goes to live in this community, it was a unique opportunity to experience this part of black history. "Obviously, *The Patriot* is about Americans fighting to gain independence from the British. But at the same time it becomes a historical lesson about the fact that blacks who had eluded the institution of slavery were in America at that time living in their own free communities. It was a wonderful experience. I was so pleased that they took the time to really show the details of how blacks

were living in this particular community, to show some of the rituals, to use the materials, some of the jewelry and stones, and incorporate all of it. It's a very important lesson for a lot of people who never understood that at that period in time there were blacks who were not enslaved. There were blacks living in a very tight community where they all shared and worked together, and were able to survive and establish a society of their own."

Bush adds that while shooting, she learned a few things about the history of the freed slaves from one of the extras who still lives in the South Carolina Gullah community. "We were talking about the music, and I said that I'd noticed there were no drums.

And he said, 'Of course, that was a deliberate move not to play the drums because they did not want the masters to know where they were located because then they would make sure that the other slaves could have no contact. Once they escaped and got to this place, of course, they could hide within and become a part of the community.'"

This Gullah Maroon becomes an oasis not only for the freed slaves but also for the traumatized Martin family. Benjamin Martin's oldest son, Gabriel, marries his sweetheart, Anne, there and Benjamin and Charlotte too share an affectionate moment. Even their garb becomes freer. Gone are the stiff corsets and high-collared coats – plus, occasionally, a little historical accuracy.

"This place represented a respite for everyone. It was almost a little bit of a fantasy. A wedding takes place here, people fall in love, so we exaggerated the wardrobe a bit to emphasize that," says costume designer Deborah Scott. "But, overall, the clothes were based on fairly authentic patterns and fabrics of the period. We imagined that the escaped and freed slaves would wear clothes that they had brought from, say, when they were working on a plantation, or garments they had found along the way. So we had a mixture of things…someone wearing a simple dress with a pair of interesting shoes that possibly she found somewhere or borrowed from someone else. We based the overall look of what freed men and slaves were wearing from paintings of the period. But we took a lot of license so that we could convey the feeling of the scenes. We had to compensate for the location as well, because it was littered with shells and very hard on the feet. So we had to invent shoes and sandals which may not have been histor-ically correct."

The scenes shot at Edisto Beach were the last to include Martin's children. Young Skye McCole Bartusiak planned to give director Roland Emmerich a very special parting gift: her fake front teeth. The actress wore a specially designed set of dentures to cover up the gaping holes left by the loss of her baby teeth and she was more than happy to reclaim her own perforated grin.

SET DECORATING

In addition to its full-time staff, the set decorating department employed over 35 artisans and crafts people to manufacture reproductions in several trades, including seven tentsmiths, six upholsterers, five candlemakers, three blacksmiths, three quiltmakers, three flag manufacturers, two tinsmiths, two basketmakers, as well as floral designers, calligraphers, taxidermists, food stylists, sculptors, paper manufacturers, etc.

In addition to what was purchased or rented, the set decorating department manufactured over 200 different lighting fixtures in over 50 different styles, ranging from primitive iron lamps to elaborate crystal chandeliers. All were lit by candles or oil (representing fat).

The set decorating department had over 2500 hand-rolled beeswax candles made especially for the film. Double and triple wicks were braided together for a more intense flame and brighter light.

The set decorating department used over 30 miles worth of the destructive kudzu vine in the manufacturing of 300 hand-woven gabions ("entrenchment baskets") and the wrapping of 180 barrels (used to simulate hickory bark rings).

Only natural, non-synthetic materials were used in the set dressing process. These materials included but were not limited to: sinew, hemp, rawhide, kudzu, oak, poplar, hickory, hay, straw, pine straw, leather, sweetgrass, canvas, burlap and muslin.

All drapery and upholstery fabrics used in the film were documented reproduction prints from the period. Mattresses were made of burlap, linen and period ticking and stuffed with corn husks, raw cotton or moss.

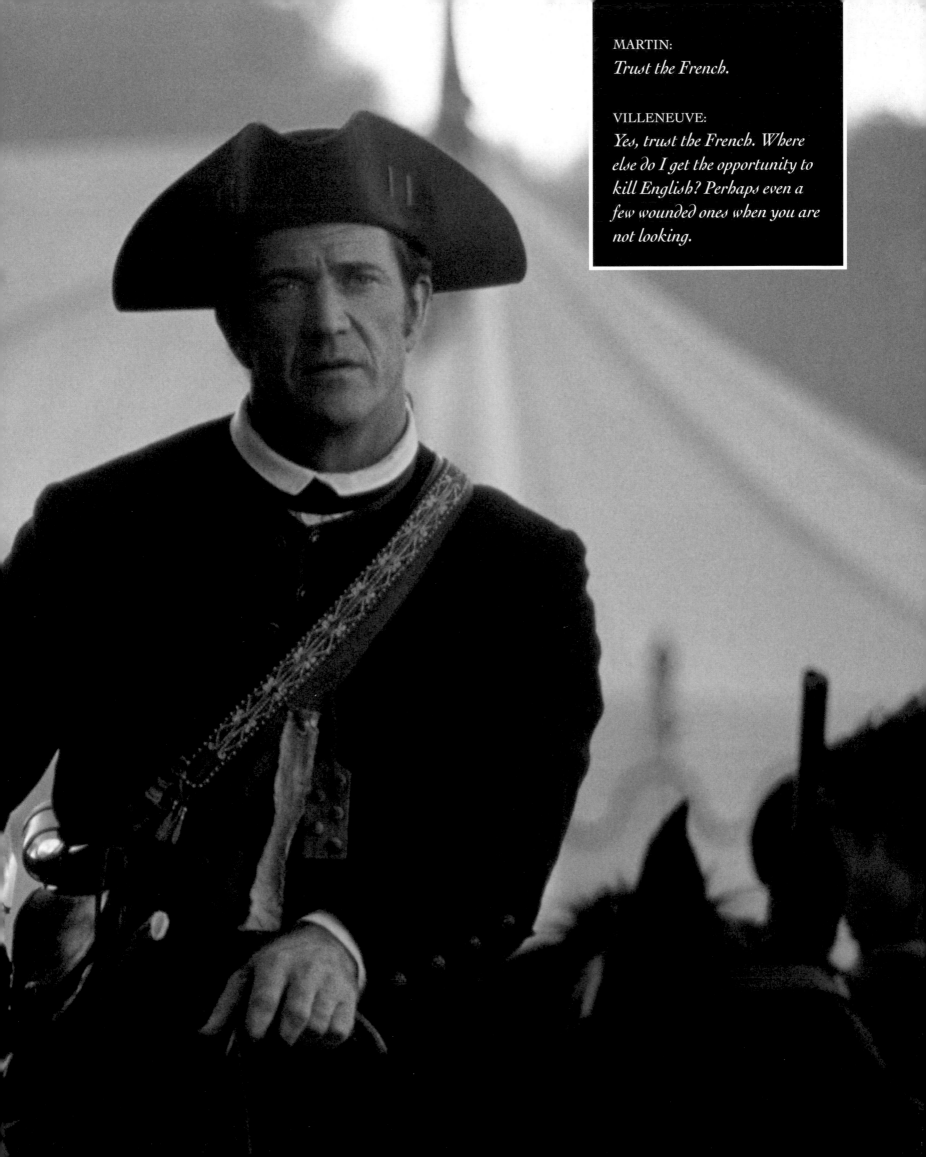

MARTIN:
Trust the French.

VILLENEUVE:
Yes, trust the French. Where else do I get the opportunity to kill English? Perhaps even a few wounded ones when you are not looking.

ACTION!

The scenes of conflict and battle are among the most dramatic and powerful in *The Patriot*. They also presented some of the greatest challenges the crew had to face.

Conflagation

The punishing fires the British set in *The Patriot* required an immense amount of planning and technique. The blaze that razed Martin's house, filmed in one shot, required six cameras and many rehearsals of extras. First, the British marched a line of somber prisoners away from the plantation; then the Green Dragoons took torches to the house and swiftly rode down the path away from the inferno, as strategically placed cameras, in cranes and on platforms, filmed the terrible event. Prior to the total destruction of the house, several "controlled" burns were accomplished, so that Emmerich could film close-ups of specific British soldiers setting fire to various parts of the structure.

The burning of the church in the village of Pembroke posed different challenges, mostly due to the effects of Hurricane Floyd. While the production luckily dodged most of the storm's devastation, it was cursed by the mercurial weather left in the hurricane's wake. After days of waiting for the rain to stop, the production finally decided to shoot the scene anyway. The dark skies and drizzle augmented the ominous tone of the sequence in which the Dragoons, under the command of Tavington, lock the townspeople of Pembroke inside the church and burn them alive. Unfortunately, by the end of the day, the shower turned into a downpour. Not only did this drench the crew and generally set a miserable atmosphere, it didn't match anything that had been filmed earlier in the day. The production had to table the church burn until the next overcast day. Naturally, the sun reappeared and it seemed the rain had taken a permanent vacation. The assistant directors had a weather service fax them updates on a regular basis and director Roland Emmerich became a devotee of the Weather Channel. Finally, a forecast for clouds emerged. The crew assembled at the church at dawn, with fire trucks and hoses ready. As the production set up, the morning gloom began to give way to yet another perfectly sunny day. Chagrined but not defeated, the company packed up and traveled to the local YMCA, where a "sun cover set" (an alternative shooting set) had been erected. Filming proceeded there until the early afternoon, when, everyone noticed, the clouds began to mass above. After a brief discussion, Emmerich decided to try to burn the church. The cast and crew hastily packed up the trucks and vans and dashed back to the church set. Their torches held aloft, the grim Green Dragoons circled the

chapel and, finally, on cue, solemnly ignited it. The thick layer of clouds above broke slightly as night fell, allowing pink streaks of sunset to peek through, catching glimmering embers that wafted through the air like fireflies as the classic colonial clapboard structure caved in and its elegant steeple toppled.

"That weather was really a stroke of luck," says first assistant director Kim Winther. "Because we had tried to shoot it for a couple days (when we thought it would be cloudy), we had rehearsed it enough. So when we finally got that overcast sunset that Roland wanted, we were prepared. We scrambled over and burned it at the magic hour."

The Battle of Camden

Filming the Camden battle sequence proved to be a challenge for all concerned. Shot over the course of two hot days, this was the first major battle scene that the production tackled. It was an impressive sight, with about 200 British and Continental forces marching towards each other, flags fluttering, the fife and drum playing plaintively as muskets and mortars exploded. The vast field was speckled with blue, yellow, red, orange and green placards, each one denoting a different-intensity explosion. Special effects coordinator Yves De Bono concocted a mixture of black powder, peat moss, and cork to place in the mortar pans buried beneath these colorful markers to simulate the effects of bursting cannonballs, and detonated the bombs on Emmerich's cue. By the end of the two days, a fine gritty layer of peat moss covered the entire company and little plugs of cork littered the grass.

One of Jason Isaacs', who plays Colonel Tavington, most embarrassing film moments occurred in front of his troops, as well as the entire film crew, during the Battle of Camden, which took place in a vast wheat field in Chester County. As the British and American forces clash, a squadron of Dragoons charge through the middle, bombs exploding around them, and their appearance leads to the Continentals' retreat. Gamely, Isaacs insisted on leading his Dragoons astride a giant horse that, unfortunately, panicked when the gunfire discharged too closely.

"When I auditioned, they asked me, 'Can you ride?' and I said, 'Of course, I'm an actor.' All actors are horse experts until they have to get on the bloody thing. I'd ridden in movies before, but then I got cast, and as it got closer, I looked at the script and I thought, 'I don't have to just trot up to a mark. I have to speed in like a bullet train into a giant crowd of people and skid the horse round in a circle and start hacking people to pieces and then gallop off again. So I panicked a bit and I thought, well, maybe I should just brush up on the riding. They brought me out three weeks early and I rode horses every morning and I shot and

BATTLE OF CAMDEN

On August 16, 1780, the Americans experienced one of their greatest setbacks. Following the fall of Charleston, South Carolina, to the British in May 1780, the American general Horatio Gates retaliated, hoping to weaken the British hold upon South Carolina. He attacked the British stronghold at the town of Camden, South Carolina, with a force of 1400 regulars and more than 2000 militia. But with his army worn down by hunger and dysentery, Gates was surprised north of Camden by General Charles Cornwallis and a British force of 2200 men. The inexperienced colonial militia fled at the first attack and the regulars were soon surrounded and nearly wiped out. This win paved the way for a subsequent British invasion of North Carolina.

The Americans suffered more than 2000 casualties, while only 324 British were killed at Camden. The battle cemented the reputation of Cornwallis but ruined the career of Gates, who was subsequently replaced.

of professional and personal concern. I stood up, because there was this amazing amount of adrenalin going through me. I would have been fine if all my bones were broken and my leg was sticking out through my ear, because there was so much adrenalin in my body. I just leapt straight back on to the horse and pretended it didn't happen. The next day, I was in terrible pain. I was very lucky, though."

Jason Isaacs grew fond of his "troops" while fighting the battle sequences and he and Jamieson Price, who played Dragoon Commander Borden, occasionally treated their Dragoons to dinner after filming. The Dragoons were played by "re-enactors" whose hobby it is to act out events from the Revolutionary War and who have a wealth of knowledge about the period.

"They were very interesting men who had very idiosyncratic lives apart from their re-enacting. They were lawyers and teachers who also had this hobby. They were very generous with their knowledge, time, and spirit and were fascinating people in general," Isaacs says.

The respect was obviously mutual. When shooting the scene in which the Pembroke church is set alight, these re-enactors galloped to safety, near the crane hoisting the camera, reined their horses into a semicircle and called for their "commanders" – Tavington and Borden. Isaacs and Price, also on horseback, trotted over. The Dragoons saluted them and acknowledged the honor it had been to "serve" them. They presented Isaacs and Price with tokens of their collective esteem: an engraved silver chalice for Isaacs and an inscribed silver shot glass for Price.

loaded muskets and pistols in the afternoon and did some saber work. I didn't fall at all during training and then the one time I did, there were 600 people on set. They'd given me this huge android of a horse. I was galloping at full pace into the two lines of British and Americans and the soldiers had gotten the wrong instructions somehow. Just as I came alongside them, yelling, 'Charge,' they fired their muskets. The horse stopped and I went flying off. There were 100 horses behind me and they all had to skid to a stop. I saw the rushes [dailies] later and all these people came tearing toward me with very worried expressions, a mixture

The Battle of Cowpens

The Americans lost the Battle of Camden and, in a way, so did the film crew of *The Patriot*. Like their predecessors, however, the production learned from the Camden defeat and used the experience to good effect at the victorious Battle of Cowpens.

"Originally, when I met with Roland, we discussed various strategies about how to shoot the battle scenes," Kim Winther recalls. "One way of going was to take all of our extras and train them, which we did. The other scenario was to rehearse them for a period of a week or two, and we did that. The other choice was to rehearse with the cameras for a couple days so that everyone would know what we were doing. Unfortunately, we could not do that, due to the time it would take and the cost of it. The Camden battle, which took place over a period of two days with lots of cameras [six] made us realize that without really rehearsing specifically for each camera, a very low percentage of shots were actually good. It was hard to time all the cameras with all the elements – smoke, gunfire, extras marching, explosions, horses – so that every camera angle was good. So we changed that philosophy for Cowpens. We used limited cameras, only two or three, not six, and set up each shot step by step, rehearsing and filming each part. That worked very well. We planned each shot for itself and, with that pace in mind, we were able to film the battle in sequence over the course of several weeks. We were able to put together all the pieces of the battle footage, with the dialogue and stunts and explosions and marching. So in some crazy way, even though Camden wasn't the success we wanted, it taught us a lot about how to shoot a battle if you don't rehearse for the cameras. We realized we couldn't really move around that quickly. It was like turning a big wheel.

"In many ways, like Francis Marion, we didn't do it the British way, we did it the American way, which was to do it in 'guerrilla' fashion. Each day we'd decide what we wanted to shoot. We made sure we had all the weapons and the mortars and the personnel, and we went from there and we were able to get what we wanted. It wasn't really regimented, we didn't rehearse and rehearse and try to attack the entire battle at once. We just approached it [incrementally], gaining more ground each day."

Emmerich's film mantra is "shooting is the best rehearsal," so this "guerrilla" approach, with its minimal drills and cameras, suited his style. The Battle of Cowpens took place on 550 acres of rolling hills and valleys, all situated on one cattle farm. The attenuated 72-foot Akelacrane was a regular visitor to the location, swinging it's arm over the British, Continental and militia forces and pivoting its extended camera to capture various angles of the battle. "It has an arm that puts you right in the middle of the action. The long arm let us sweep across the militia to reveal the enemy troops they would be fighting. A great example of this is when Benjamin and the militia charge the ruins and overrun the British," Caleb Deschanel, Director of Photography, says. "What we tried to do was put the audience in to the battles and give them the same sense of awe and terror as the troops. We wanted to create a sense of what warfare was like then because today you don't see the enemy up close."

More traditional cameras, on dolly tracks and up on stilts, also shot various positions. Transporting all this gear, as well as the usual film support stuff, from additional lenses to craft services, required military-style organization and every department had a fleet of all-terrain vehicles, known as mules, to deliver the necessary items quickly over occasionally inhospitable terrain. The British and American encampments, for instance, were literally miles apart and while vans conveyed personnel from location to location, the more nimble and speedy mules proved more practical in terms of delivering equipment. Even they were restricted, however, as Emmerich did not want any of the vehicles to leave distinctly contemporary tire tracks.

Apart from the principal actors, the most important participants in the Cowpens battle were the background artists, playing the soldiers themselves, as many as 600 on certain days. A unique mixture of re-enactors, stunt people, and extras, they trained together in boot camp prior to filming to learn how to portray an eighteenth-century warrior.

· 85 ·

"We had a three-tiered group, with the re-enactors, trained extras, and extras. Our approach was that we would use a certain percentage out of the re-enactor community, people who would come with their own guns, their own knowledge of the period, and proper drill techniques, and then we would supplement that with extras. We would send people through a training camp and teach them to use the weapons, and they would be our primary extras. Then, on our biggest battle days, we would bring in people whom we did not specifically train but we would wardrobe them, put them in the

Director of Photography Caleb Deschanel (left) with Emmerich and Gibson

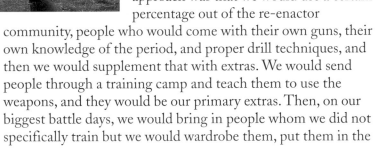

BATTLE OF COWPENS

On January 17, 1781, in a brilliant defeat over British forces on the northern border of South Carolina, American troops and militia slowed General Cornwallis' campaign to invade North Carolina.

Daniel Morgan was sent with 1000 troops to the south-west to intercept Cornwallis' advance. When confronted at Cowpens with 1150 troops under Colonel Banastre Tarleton, Morgan delivered a serious and surprising blow. The British were hit hard with 600 casualties, while the Americans lost only seventy-two men. Tarleton escaped with 140 horsemen but his reputation was gone and he rejoined Cornwallis as nothing more than a good cavalry officer. The value of the American victory at Cowpens was that it ended northern apathy to the situation in the south, resulting in the military assistance needed to achieve independence. Had the north ignored the situation in the south, the regiments that brought Cornwallis down at Yorktown might not have been successful.

background and they would sort of follow what the other people did," says the re-enactor coordinator Riley Flynn. "Boot camp was conducted for two weeks in total. Each individual went only for a week but we had 100 people during the first week and another 100 during the second. They were taught principally to use the weapons. We were dealing with a flintlock weapon, a weapon which is ignited by flint striking a piece of metal and causing a spark, which is a technique and an art. Learning to march and do the proper drill, and to obey the commands of the period, were all part of it, as well as a bit of stunt training, under the direction of R. A. Rondell, the stunt coordinator, so that they could do some close-up battle scenes, such as charging someone with a bayonet."

Flynn scoured the country for these re-enactors. Often they came with their own horses and guns, and many elected to live the part, camping out in a sprawling suburb of tents that sprang up near the Cowpens location. They also arrived with their own specific knowledge of the period, some of which was not always conducive to filming. A scene in which the Dragoons storm over the hill into a force of Americans, who charge in return, did not work as planned, primarily because the Continental forces were so busy reciting the historical formal commands and ritualized movements that the British were upon them before they could react. On the next try, the assistant directors adjusted the timing and omitted some of the commands.

While this might not have been "historically accurate" to some of the re-enactors, Flynn is philosophical. "History is a judgement and it evolves. The same is true of the re-enactments. What we hoped to do on this project was to present the period and to be honest to it. But we may not always be specifically honest in all of the tactics. For instance, some of our cannons were properly designed cannons from the period but were probably too big to have been used on the type of battle that we depicted. But we didn't use machine-guns. And I can go to any re-enactment in the country and find people with eyeglasses fighting, people who are overweight or too old. I will find 'units' in which there are only four people in the same uniform. This is not historically correct. Besides, I always say that if you rub two re-enactors together, you will get an argument over authenticity. And I think they all learned a lot from the project. For instance, all the horsemen never had more than four horses together before and I had them doing drills with twenty to forty horses. Many of the re-enactors had never worked with mortars before," he says.

Stunt coordinator R. A. Rondell had to ensure that the Battle of Cowpens was not only historically accurate, in terms of the way his team fought, but also exciting to watch and safely executed. "It was organized chaos, trying to create a battle scene in some kind of control. I brought in about thirty-five or forty of the stunt people from Los Angeles, plus we worked with 400 and 500 local people, re-enactors from all over the country that all bring their own expertise to the project. And then we tried to train them as one to be one complete team. There were four offensive moves they used with the rifle, four different blocks, and a lunge, and six offensive moves, which were swipes across the face, swipes across the body, and lunges with the bayonet and the butt of the rifle at the face. They took those sequences and maybe added a few of their own little fight routines, a jab or a slash, so that they weren't all fighting exactly the same. It was actually a big dance and the moves were all originally taught in the Marine Corps. They've been around since well before the Revolutionary War, from what I understand, and are still in use today."

The idea was to create quasi-stunt people, augmented by the real things, because in the course of filming, the men could never be sure who their opponent would be. "What happens when you line up 400 or 500 guys in a line on both sides of the fields, 200 yards apart, and then they go to hand-to-hand combat and come running across the field at each other, the chances of them meeting up with the exact partner they practiced with are slim to none. Nobody's got the same timing, nobody's got the same pace. So when they clashed, once they broke loose one guy might be quicker than the next and he'd end up with a totally new adversary, maybe one he never rehearsed with. So it started to look messy, like a real battle. And that's what we wanted. It was supposed to be chaos, but it was controlled chaos because everybody knew the moves," he says.

The most important fight of this sequence, of course, was the one between Martin and Tavington. Gibson and Isaacs worked closely with Rondell and their stunt doubles to choreograph this elaborate struggle and the actors often skipped lunch to practice and improvise. Like two little boys, the pair came up with increasingly gruesome routines, enthusiastically demonstrating them for director Roland Emmerich. When it came time to shoot the scene, it actually took place over several days and both men, bloodied and bruised, nonchalantly walked around set with swords and bayonets sticking "through" their bodies.

Gabriel's Rescue

In addition to the major battles of Camden and Cowpens, *The Patriot* featured several pivotal "skirmishes," such as the sequence known as "Gabriel's Rescue". Shot on 1000-acre wooded expanse full of beeches, red and white oaks, cotton woods and gum trees, with ten springs, two lakes, and a plethora of indigenous animals, including deer and wild turkey, the property resembled land the colonists might have settled. The topography perfectly suited the scene. A high ridge overlooked a path and stream, along which came the British convoy of soldiers, wagons and prisoners, including Martin's captured son Gabriel. Above, Martin and his younger boys waited like snipers, aiming their long rifles at the advancing Redcoats. Trevor Morgan and Bryan Chafin, who played Martin's sons, decided that their characters were sharpshooters who would have also served in the militia had they been older. While their characters approach their murderous assignment with grim trepidation, both Morgan and Chafin eagerly anticipated the moment when they would actually fire their guns.

The scene was also Gibson's first opportunity to demonstrate his prowess with the musket. Concealing rifles behind trees, he sprinted from trunk to trunk, firing and reloading with ease. Tearing down the hillside, he then moved on to the tomahawk. Working with his stunt double, Lance Gilbert, and R. A. Rondell, Gibson performed a harrowing dance of death, hacking and maiming his opponents. Of course, all this mayhem took place over several days and the British "died" beautifully: a gunshot to the head knocked one off his horse; a slit throat claimed another. Gibson, on the run, hurled his tomahawk into a retreating Redcoat, its macabre speed and deadly effects accented by the whip pan of the camera. Gibson's goal, of course, was to hurl the tomahawk perilously close to his adversary but not to actually hurt him, since the weapon was real. (The rubber version didn't have the heft to sail through the air and, worse, in close-ups the lightweight material wobbled.) On one take, his aim was a little more accurate than he anticipated – fortunately, no bodily parts were lost.

SPECIAL AND VISUAL EFFECTS

Mechanical and Makeup Effects

In *The Patriot*'s battle scenes, the mechanical effects team was responsible for everything from smoke to bullet hits to cannon fire while the make-up special effects team reproduced the inevitable wounds and fatalities such weapons cause.

The mechanical team constructed fully functional field and siege cannons that fired large charges of explosives, also created by these technicians. In fact, the team manufactured and detonated 4000 simulated cannon explosives, using 9000 feet of detonating cord and two tons of black powder. Once built, these steel cannons were covered by the mold-making department with a fiberglass and plaster shell to be painted and detailed with the final touches of authenticity. To better track the impact of the cannons on screen, over 10,000 bags of peat moss were used to maximize their impact. The team, led by special effects coordinator Yves De Bono, also created a high-speed cannon ball rig, which enabled a cannon ball secured to a cable to safely pass near actual amputees who had fake limbs attached, while adhering to the strictest safety guidelines, of course. According to special effects technician Mark Griffin, "in the scene, it will appear as if these soldiers have had their limbs torn off as the cannon ball hurls past." The special effects make-up team also had a hand in this scene, including the leg itself that went flying in a spray of blood.

Another effective contribution of De Bono's team were the magnesium guns which were usually fired during dusk or night scenes. Co-producer and second unit director Peter Winther recalls that "the magnesium flash guns illuminated everything, really lit up the night sky. It juxtaposed a beautiful image with the violence of war. The guns helped tie this together."

In another joint effort, two mechanical "horses" were created by the mechanical and make-up special effects departments to perform a number of thankless or hazardous tasks, including crashing into walls and becoming the target of cannon fire. Horse sculptor Bruce Larsen, based his creations on those that the Dragoons rode, with each muscle sculpted to move and react

like a real horse. Once the sculpture was completed, Larsen and technician Brent Connelly molded the horses in fiberglass. A metal frame was then made by Ron Colucci in the mechanical department to fit inside the mold so that the foam would bend and move right once it filled up the mold. Larsen then pieced the horse together and "furred" it with a spandex-based fur. These "horses" were perfectly suited to run down a track, launch off and fall in a realistic manner.

In addition to the mechanical horses, the make-up team, led by Bill "Splat" Johnson, created various prosthetic wounds, body parts, dummies and an uncanny set of George Washington prosthetics. A crew of no more than five people at any given time created nearly one hundred effects for the film.

Following initial production meetings with Emmerich, director of photography Caleb Deschanel and De Bono, Johnson created various conceptual drawings. Medical books were used for accuracy of wounds and internal anatomy. Once sculpted and molded, silicone pieces were made and painted to match the references and actors. Generic silicone wounds were sewn onto spandex sleeves and shirts that could be worn under wardrobe. These gave the illusion of realistic wounds, but took no time to apply. Various types of blood were created. Some types were made that would stay on all day and not run while others were made to show various stages of coagulation.

Perhaps the most challenging task for the make-up effects team was to create one of our country's most recognized faces-that of George Washington. Creating the George Washington make-up was Johnson's favorite effect, requiring extensive research. He attended an exhibit, which displayed a sculpture based on an actual cast of Washington's face, as well as a cast of his false teeth. Actor Terry Layman, who portrayed America's first president in the film, had a mold made of his head and teeth. Using photographs taken at the exhibit as reference, Johnson sculpted on the cast of Layman's face. Molds were then made of the sculpture and latex foam pieces were created. Key special effects make-up artist Corey Castellano created a dental appliance to broaden the actor's face and the hair department supplied a wig and sideburns. Making the effect even more challenging was the fact that the entire scene was shot in daylight, which is unforgiving to prosthetic make-up. But Johnson was able to match the skintones of the actor, creating a natural look, even the under the strongest sunlight. Co-producer and second unit director Peter Winther remembers that "Terry's face was pretty angular and George Washington's was rounder, so they put these pumps in his cheeks that he could activate himself . He looked just like the portrait on the dollar bill which is what Roland was asking for."

The digital effects, which were created primarily in post-production at Centropolis Effects (CFX) in Culver City, California, presented an entirely different set of obstacles to overcome. Visual effects producer Fiona Stone describes their goal as "absolutely subtle. Hopefully the audience will be in awe that they are being transported back to a time 200 years ago but they won't be thinking, 'oh yeah, that was created by effects.' They'll be so in tune with the story it will all be subliminal to them." Thousands of soldiers were ever so "subtlety" created and placed on the battlefields for Camden and Cowpens, as well as eighteenth-century ships in the harbor and city of Charles Town and dozens upon dozens of battle action enhancements.

Visual Effects

Led by Academy Award®-winning visual effects supervisor Stuart Robertson, the visual effects work created for the battle scenes of *The Patriot* began with one man, actually one soldier. In order to have scenes with thousands of soldiers, and still have ultimate control over all of the action in the shot, it was necessary for the team to create a single digital model. The computer-generated modeling team, led by Bret St. Clair, created the digital soldier model by combining multiple shapes and surfaces to represent a soldier in full Revolutionary War attire. These 3D surfaces were then textured (a process that attaches 2D digital paintings onto the 3D surfaces) to provide a further level of realism that would not be otherwise achievable. Once the surface model was complete, it was then combined with a virtual skeleton – a system of bones and joints that correspond to those of a human skeleton. With the surfaces attached to the skeleton, it could be moved or animated over time to give the appearance of life-like movement. Once the original model was fully tested, several variations of the model were then created to provide a diverse appearance among the digital soldiers. Since each army had very few variations of dress, only four variations of digital models were necessary. However, the militia models proved a heady undertaking with upwards of 20 variations created to appropriately match their ragtag diversity.

The next major step in the set-up process was to create a library of movement or animation for these soldiers to perform. In order to achieve the most realistic human movement, the team utilized the technique of "Performance Motion Capture", courtesy of House of Moves L.L.C. and Elektrashock Inc. facilities in Los Angeles. To take realism to the next level, CFX employed a Revolutionary War re-enactor to march, shoot, reload and die. A series of infrared lights and cameras were used to capture the movement of tracking markers from different points of view, while specialized software was used to recreate the movement on the computer. The "captured" movements of the re-enactor were then applied to the skeleton of the digital model, giving its surfaces the same realistic movement.

Since this collection of captured movement data needed to be combined in a multitude of different ways for different shots, the next part of the set-up phase was to manipulate this data in a way that would make it possible to seamlessly blend one movement into another, or to blend a single movement with itself to make it loopable. In this way, a two-second motion capture of the re-enactor walking could be looped to create an endless walk cycle.

While digital model and motion capture libraries were being created, a tool was developed by CFX software developer Fabrice Ceugniet, which could "spray" or spread large numbers of soldiers of different heights and varying animations and walking cycles throughout a given visual effects shot. In later versions of this highly specialized tool, it was even possible for the soldiers to walk over hilly terrain. This proprietary spray tool was integrated into the 3D animation software package called Maya (from Alias/Wavefront), which was used for all digital modeling and motion capture blending needs.

The first step of the digital effects process is to take the original film negative and scan (digitize) it into the computer. Once the filmed elements exist on the computer as a series of pixels, the process can begin. Once the digital imagery is complete, these computer-based images are then recorded back out to film frame-by-frame as a new original negative.

With the live-action background or "plate" elements scanned and placed online, the digital effects process for each shot can proceed with both the 3D or modeling and animation team, and 2D or compositing team, beginning their work on the shot concurrently.

A digital photograph taken at the Motion Capture stage shoot showing the tracking marker balls attached to a Revolutionary War re-enactor. The maker balls are used to record the re-enactor's joint movements over time in 3D space

3D - Camera Tracking (Match Moving)

The first step in the process of integrating 3D computer-generated elements into a live-action scene is to track or match the movement of the camera that took place during the filming of the shot with a 3D "virtual" camera move. Without having the computer camera perfectly matched to the live-action camera, the 3D-rendered soldiers or other 3D elements will appear to slip or slide against the background plate – thereby defying the illusion of reality.

3D camera tracking relies on measuring selected landmarks, or static points, that appear in the photographed scene – for example, window corners and another architectural details, or large markers set by the crew. The changing shapes of these landmarks, as the camera moves past them, allows the tracker to back-engineer the camera's path in space and time, and feed that camera information to the digital (or motion-control) camera. Plate tracking supervisor Archie Gogoladze, recalls that "I was running back and forth with this eight foot marker on my shoulders, just trying to make the shot when I would hear, 'get ready and roll sound,' so I would just lay down in the grass not to be seen and wait for the shot to pass before jumping back up and running out of the way. I lost 15 pounds and it was a great experience!"

CFX had honed its tracking techniques on the huge *Godzilla* project, which was shot entirely without mechanical encoding equipment, in the strongly geometrical environment of downtown Manhattan. The geometry of the city, regular and permanent, furnishes a wealth of shapes to provide ready-made tracking points. The team faced a different challenge on the set of *The Patriot*, where the natural locations of open fields and mile-wide cow pastures didn't supply the geometrical survey clues of the city, and therefore demanded a reliance on fluorescent pink, eight foot high markers.

As a backup, satellite mapping data of each site provided by the United States Geological Survey were used to give, to give us the overall topography of each location. Finally, camera moves were recorded with an electronic encoding system, custom-made by General Lift Inc., for the primary camera crane.

With the information derived from these systems, and with the background plates at hand, tracking supervisor Aimee Campbell and the tracking team completed the process for each shot using both highly specialized software and time consuming hand tracking techniques to ensure that our 3D elements would appear locked to the background plate.

3D - Soldier Blocking

In *The Patriot*, battlefield scenes comprised the vast majority of shots in which 3D elements were integrated into the live-action background plates. For each of these shots, the first step was to create a rough "blocking" pass in order to solicit feedback on troop placement and movement from Stuart Robertson and Emmerich. This shot blocking was achieved through the use of CFX's in-house troop placement tool, which was developed by Fabrice Ceugniet and overseen by computer graphics supervisor Thomas Dadras. Although the primary purpose of this tool was to allow the individual 3D animators to place battalions of fully textured 3D soldier models into a battlefield scene, it was also designed to first allow the animators to represent these digital soldiers as a series of simple cylindrical shapes. Since the animating and rendering of hundreds or thousands of highly detailed soldiers was a time consuming process, this technique made it possible to quickly render and present the shot layout for feedback. Dadras admits that "since we knew that the soldiers were going to be seen in the distance, we ended up taking pictures of ourselves and people in the company to apply as texture, giving some kind of detail so the soldiers don't look like flesh-colored blobs. Still, it won't be possible for my mom to recognize me."

3D - Battlefield Choreography

Once the initial "blocking" for a given shot was approved, the 3D animator could proceed with the placement of the fully textured 3D soldiers into the scene. With the rough placement and movement of the soldiers already worked out, the choreography phase, led by Dadras, animation supervisor Kelvin Lee and sequence supervisor Paolo Moscatelli, was focused more on what the different groups of soldiers were doing in different areas of the battlefield scene. Since the immense amount of 3D soldier model data required of these scenes was too large for even the most powerful of graphics workstations to handle, each shot needed to be broken down into a series of "soldier layers", ranging from 7 to 21 layers per shot. The 3D animators could then work with these more manageable layers to choreograph the action required. Each layer would eventually be rendered separately and combined later during the 2D compositing portion of the process.

3D - Lighting & Rendering

With the placement and movement of the digital soldiers having been worked out, the next step in the process was to digitally "light" the scene which Lee and Moscatelli also managed. Since the 3D soldiers were typically placed right next to or behind the actual soldiers in the scene, the animators needed to carefully work on the placement and color of the virtual lights, as well as fine-tune the colors of the textures that were applied to the soldier models to give them the same appearance as their human counterparts. Dadras explains, "Since the live-action plates were filmed in broad daylight, the primary light source of the virtual scene needed to emulate the color, light angle and intensity of the sun. With the sunlight and cloud coverage changing during the filming of every shot, this virtual lighting needed to be changed and fine-tuned for each and every shot." The animators were then ready to render the layers in preparation for the compositing phase. The rendering process is where the computer is used to generate flat 2D "photographic" images of the 3D virtual scene using the tracked virtual camera as the point of view for the "photos".

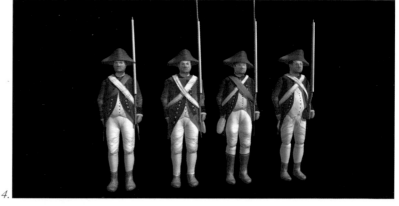

1.   2.   3.   4.

3D – Effects Animation

Along with the digital soldier elements that were created, many other digital effects elements were produced to help enhance the reality of each shot. Among these were computer-generated cannon balls, musket smoke, flags, water and cannonball trails. The effects animation team, led by Nickson Fong, used a variety of techniques and software to achieve a level of realism that would allow these additional elements to help bring the shots to life.

2D – Paint/Rotoscoping

Throughout the wide spectrum of challenges that were faced on the visual effects work for *The Patriot*, there was a tremendous need for paint, a frame-by-frame digital photo retouching, and rotoscoping work, a frame-by-frame process in which the digital artists literally create cutouts of actors, trees, building, etc. from the live-action plates so that these different elements can be later combined with one another during the compositing phase of the shot. The paint & roto team, led by Robert Cribbett, was charged with the painstaking task of painting and rotoscoping tens of thousands of individual film frames which included painting out wires, tracking markers, trees, actors, cameramen, cameras, dollys and even dolly tracks in order to achieve a clean usable background plate.

2D – Soldier Cloning

With inherent visual limitations as to how close the 3D digital soldier models could be placed in front of the camera, a technique known as 2D cloning was utilized in some shots to replicate soldiers required in the foreground areas. In this technique, the soldiers in the live-action background plates were literally cut out in the rotoscoping phase, and then repositioned and pasted back into the same background plate giving the illusion that the shot was filmed with many more soldiers than were actually present. In most cases, these "cloned" soldiers were then further combined with the 3D digital soldier elements to complete the layout of the battlefield scenes.

2D – Compositing

The final phase in the digital effects process lies in the hands of the compositing team whose task it is to combine all of the elements into a seamless image. Each element of a given shot,

Above, from left:
1) A wireframe representation of a single digital soldier model
2) A flat shaded view illustrating the 3D surfaces that make up the soldier model
3) A fully rendered view, showing how 2D texture mapping techniques were used to augment the level of detail of the soldier model
4) Four digital soldier models. Minor variations between the models help to provide a diverse appearance for the soldiers when used repeatedly in a shot

Below, from top:
1) A battalion of soldiers including drummers and flag carriers as created by 3D animator Eric Tablada. A proprietary in-house soldier placement or "spray" tool was used to attach slightly randomized movement to the individual soldiers to give the battalion a life-like appearance

2) The original background plate showing the live-action soldiers and pyrotechnic effects that were filmed on location in South Carolina

1.

2.

3.

3) The finished shot as composited by 2D artist Doug Tubach showing digital soldiers layered into the live-action smoke

Step one: original photography on location in Charleston, South Carolina

whether live-action, computer-generated (CG), or model against a green screen is layered together with numerous adjustments made to depth, contrast and focus. In the case of *The Patriot*, the layer of computer-generated soldiers posed a particular challenge as they appear side-by-side the actual actors and at a much closer proximity to the camera than has been done in the past. Compositing supervisor Conny Fauser explains "when placing a CG soldier right next to an actual actor, you can see all the subtle differences between them. From the color intensity and light play on the glints of the rifles, to the differences in color between uniforms, boots, hats, cuffs, etc., it's the compositor's job to find ways to eliminate those differences and make the CG incorporation seamless. If the [CG] soldiers are walking through the grass, you have to make their steps look realistic by adding the shadows and the little things no one thinks about unless those details aren't there. There's no cheating because the digital soldiers are standing right next to the real guys."

Soldiers and battle scenes were just one of the challenges the compositors faced, as wide shots of eighteenth-century Charles Town and Yorktown were included to "sell" the time period and tell the story. Visual effects supervisor Stuart Robertson explains that part of the city street scene would be shot on location and the shot "…about 30 feet wide. On the right, the street was 'dressed' with people historically costumed and street vendors milling around, then on the left, everything was later digitally replaced with ships and houses of the time." Robertson collaborates with Emmerich regarding what is shot live-action and what is created via model and digital effects. He then mocks up initial storyboards and gives each team their respective assignments. Wide cityscapes were included to help illustrate the many changes that Charles Town underwent throughout the course of the war. Artist Michael Lloyd was hired specifically to create these images as digital or "matte" paintings, which combine actual photography with additional photography and reference material.

Step two: Nineteenth- and twentieth-century buildings are removed from the plate

Miniatures models were relied on for many of the period details, such as the ships. Robertson explains, "It's more efficient to create a scale model where you can pay attention to all of these intricate details." The models and the miniatures of the harbor environments and the huge sailing ships were created by the Munich Visual Effects Firm of Magicon GmbH under the direction of model supervisor Joachim Grüninger.

Unlike some films where the effects teams have little to no interaction with the director and the principle photography unit, the need for seamless integration of the images called for greater interaction between teams. Compositing supervisor Nelson Sepulveda adds, "We had to think like photographers and painters at the same time. Not only were we trying to make the effects look real, but also as beautiful as Caleb's photography – no pressure!"

Fauser sums up the experience with a wish for the movie-goer's experience, "Hopefully we will create the illusion that everything was done in-camera. Audiences will be looking at a period piece but will not be able to tell what's model, what's green screen, CG or real. No one should leave the theater thinking, 'wow, there were a lot of special effects in that movie' but hopefully when they later find out what we pulled off, they will be surprised."

Step three: the models of ships and eighteenth-century buildings are added

Step four: the greenscreen shoot for the model street

Step five: the greenscreen people are added

Step six: all of the elements are put together. Still a work in progress, this is the last step before completing the shot

TIMELINE

1754–63, *French and Indian War*
France and many Indian nations unite against Britain/colonies. For years the two giants, Britain and France, have struggled for dominance in North America while engaging in guerrilla warfare with Native Americans. Britain emerges as the supreme power in North America and the French are driven out. Sugar and Stamp Acts follow.

1763
The Proclamation of 1763 prohibited colonists from settling west of the Allegheny Mountains.

1765, *Stamp Act*
Colonies are to be taxed directly without representation in Parliament. "No taxation without representation" is the angry response. The Sons of Liberty, led by Boston brewer Sam Adams, is formed in opposition to the Stamp Act, as well as Committees of Correspondence. The Act is repealed in 1766. Quartering Acts are passed, with colonies required to pay for British troops stationed there.

1766, *Townshend Acts*
A tax is applied to certain British imports, such as lead, glass, paper, paint and tea. A boycott begins immediately. Soon the colonies are doing without British goods at all.

March 5, 1770, *Boston Massacre*
Building tension erupts into violence. Colonists taunt Redcoats, shots ring out, five people in the crowd are killed and six wounded.

December 16, 1773, *Boston Tea Party*
Parliament passes the Tea Act, giving British merchants a monopoly on sale of tea to the colonies. Boston Patriots (dressed like Indians) dump tons of tea into Boston Harbor. Similar actions take place in all the colonies.

1774, *Intolerable Acts*
Boston's port is closed until the tea is paid for. Massachusetts loses the right to self-government and is placed under British rule.

September 5–October 26, 1774
First Continental Congress. All colonies except Georgia send representatives. The Congress protests against the Intolerable Acts and boycotts British trade; delegates state that Parliament in Britain has no authority to pass laws governing the colonies without consent. Parliament refuses to accept this and the colonies prepare for war.

April 19, 1775, *Battle of Lexington (Mass.):*
"The shot heard around the world." Start of the American Revolution. The British general Thomas Cage was ordered to crush the rebellion and seize colonial arms, along with leaders John Hancock and Sam Adams. William Davies, Paul Revere and William Dawes rode into countryside to alert the colonists: "The British are coming!" Minutemen ride to Lexington and Concord, where 350 British light infantrymen advance. The Minutemen retreat, keeping their weapons, and British lines open fire. No one knows who fired the first shot, but the battle lasted less than five minutes. Eight Minutemen were killed.

May 1775, *Second Continental Congress*
Congress approves the creation of an army and navy (at Marblehead, Mass.) and money is raised. George Washington is elected to command the Continental army.

June 1775, *Battle of Bunker Hill (actually Battle of Breed's Hill)*
This is the first real battle, where Washington is reported to have instructed his men, "Don't fire till you see the whites of their eyes." The British defeat the Patriots, but suffer 1000 casualties compared with the Americans' 400+. This is the bloodiest, most violent battle of the war.

July 21, 1775
Benjamin Franklin draws up a plan of confederation/perpetual union – "The United Colonies of North America". This is considered by Congress.

January 1, 1776
Washington unfurls first Union flag of thirteen stripes at Cambridge, Mass.

Prohibitory Act passed by Parliament to shut off trade with the colonies/seize all ships.

July 4, 1776
Delegates from the thirteen colonies meet in Philadelphia and issue the Declaration of Independence.

August 1776, *Battle of Long Island*
Washington withdraws his forces from Long Island to the City of New York. Congress resolves that all Continental Commissions in which the words 'United Colonies' have been used should hereafter refer to the 'United States.' The Americans evacuate New York City. The British are repulsed at Harlem Heights.

December 8, 1776
Washington crosses the Delaware into Pennsylvania.

July 31, 1777
The French general Lafayette offers his services to Congress and is commissioned Major-General.

1777, *Battle of Orsikany (NY);*
Battle of Bennington (VT); Battle of Brandywine (Penn.); Battle of Stillwater (NY)

September 27, 1777
The British army occupies Philadelphia.

November 15, 1777
The Articles of Confederation (precursor to the Constitution) are adopted.

February 6, 1778
Persuaded by Benjamin Franklin, the French King Louis XVI acknowledges the independence of the colonies and signs the Treaty of Alliance and Commerce, making the French army, navy and French money available.

Baron von Steuben joins Valley Forge camp and teaches the American troops to fight like a European army.

August 31, 1778
The Americans evacuate Rhode Island and the British occupy Newport.

December 29, 1778
The British troops under Howe capture Savannah. The Americans retreat across Savannah River.

February 14, 1779, *Battle of Kettle Creek (GA)*
American victory.

April 10, 1780
General Clinton lays siege to Charles Town.

April 14, 1780 *Battle at Monck's Corner (SC)*

May 12, 1780
Charles Town capitulates.

May 29, 1780
Massacre of Americans under Colonel Buford by British under General Banastre Tarleton at Waxhaw (NC).

June 3, 1780
Sir Henry Clinton proclaims South Carolina subject to England.

August 16, 1780, *Battle of Camden (SC)*
Gates defeated.

January 17, 1781, *Battle of Cowpens (SC)*
American victory. Daniel Morgan leads fight against General Tarleton. Morgan arranges clever ambush.

January 28–February 13, 1781 Retreat of Americans under General Greene from Cowpens to the River Dan, pursued by General Cornwallis.

October 19, 1781, *Battle of Yorktown (VA)*
British soldiers marched out of Yorktown to lay down their arms. General Cornwallis surrenders.

September 3, 1783, *Treaty of Paris*
Signed by the United States and Britain, this ends the Revolutionary War.

1787
The Constitution comes into effect, ratified by nine of the thirteen states.

1789
George Washington inaugurated as first President of the United States.

1791
The first ten amendments to the Constitution are ratified as the Bill of Rights.